Sewing With
SERGERS

THE COMPLETE HANDBOOK FOR OVERLOCK SEWING

Revised Edition

**by
Gail Brown and
Pati Palmer**

Book design & production by
Wisner Associates, Portland, Oregon.

Technical and fashion illustrations
by Kate Pryka and Carol Turner.

Divider page fashion illustrations
by Maggie Raguse.

Revised edition edit by Ann Price.

We could not have written this book without the gracious cooperation of representatives from many sewing machine companies. Our special thanks are extended to the following people and companies, listed in alphabetical order by the serger brand name they produce: Sue Green, Baby Lock (Tacony Corp.); Ann Price and Diana Schlumpf, Bernette (Bernina Sewing Machine Co. Inc.); Vicki Hastings, Combi 10 and Designer Lock (New Home Sewing Machine Company); Jonathan Pollack, Consew (Consolidated Sewing Machine Corp.); Jacqueline Toole and Elvie Tarien, Hobby Lock (Pfaff American Sales Corp.); Deb Gangnon, Donna Houtchens, LaRue Smith, Terry Smith, Husky Lock (Husquvarna Corp.—formerly Viking); Dorothy Tullam, Juki Lock (Juki Industries of America Inc.); Sue Bagley, Necchi Lock (Allyn Distributing Company—Necchi U.S.A.); Craig Neal and Sally Richman, Riccar Lock (Riccar); Donna Grant and Zoe Graul, The Singer Professional and the Ultralock (Singer Company); Becky Williams, Super Lock (White Sewing Machine Company).

In addition, we would like to thank: Dianne Giancola and Janet Klaer, Coats & Clark Inc.; Esther Randall, Y.L.I. Corp.; Gail Hamilton, McCall Pattern Company; Marta Alto, Karen Dillon, Susan Pletsch, Lynn Raasch and Leslie Wood of Palmer/Pletsch Associates; Barbara Weiland, **Sew News**; and Bobbie Keeney, who remains our most patient and proficient typist.

ABOUT THE AUTHORS...

Together, Gail Brown and Pati Palmer have over forty years of professional sewing experience. Both home economists are well known for their thorough product and technique research. In an effort to compile the most useful and up-to-date information for this book, they tested fifteen home-use sergers, including models from every major sewing machine company.

Gail Brown, a University of Washington graduate in Home Economics, took her Clothing and Textiles degree to New York where she became promotional consultant and later marketing director for one of the largest retail fabric companies. She since has been Communications Director for Stretch and Sew, Inc. She has appeard on "Sewing with Nancy" (PBS and The Learning Channel), the "Daytime" series (ABC/ Hearst), and AM Northwest (ABC, Portland, Oregon). Her Palmer/Pletsch books include: **Sewing With Sergers, Creative Serging, Sensational Silk,** and **Sew a Beautiful Wedding.** Other books include **Innovative Serging, Innovative Sewing, Quick Napkin Creations, The Super Sweater Idea Book,** and **Instant Interiors.** Gail's byline appears in many sewing publications including **Sew News** and **McCall's Pattern Magazine.** She works out of her home in Hoquiam, Washington, where she lives with her husband John Quigg and two children, Bett and Jack.

Pati Palmer, CEO of Palmer/Pletsch Publishing also designs best-selling patterns for McCall Pattern Company. She has been an educational representative for the Armo Company, Corporate Home Economist for Meier & Frank, an Oregon department store, where she taught up to ten sewing classes per week and bought sewing notions for five stores. She shares her extensive knowledge with seminar audiences throughout the United States, Canada, and Australia. A Home Economics graduate in Clothing and Textiles from Oregon State Universiy, she has served on the national board of Home Economists in Business as Public Relations Chairman and Vice-chairman of Member Relations and is a member of Fashion Group. She has co-authored the following books: **Sewing with Sergers, Creative Serging, Mother Pletsch's Painless Sewing, Pants for Any Body, Sewing Ultrasuede Brand Fabrics, The Serger Idea Book,** and **Easy, Easier, Easiest Tailoring.**

TABLE OF CONTENTS

TABLE OF CONTENTS

What is a Serger?

CHAPTER 1

WHAT IS A SERGER?

The serger, also called an overlock machine, or "overlocker," is revolutionizing sewing. It stitches, trims and overcasts in one step at almost twice the speed of a conventional sewing machine. A conventional machine sews from 700 to 1100 stitches per minute and a serger sews up to 1700 stitches per minute.

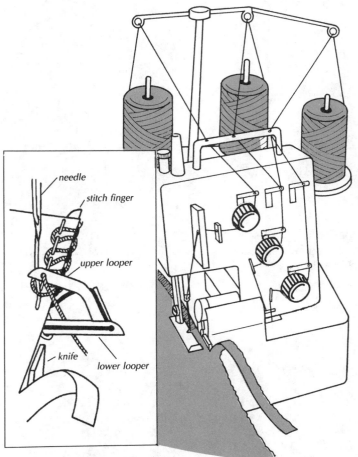

Sergers have made sewing more exciting than ever, so **watch out!** This book is full of convincing reasons why you should buy one. If you own one and want to **UPGRADE**, don't sell your first machine. True luxury is owning **TWO!!** Keep one always set up for a rolled edge or threaded with white thread! Or, use one for seam finishing while the other is set for a special decorative thread.

WHAT CAN SERGERS DO?

Sergers allow you to duplicate ready-to-wear seaming and finishing never before possible with conventional machines.

- Unlined jackets can be beautifully finished inside.

- Silks and silkies can have narrow pucker-free seams.

- Single layer ruffles and soft flared skirts can be narrow hemmed in minutes.

- You can cut and sew sweaterknit yardage and finish edges with decorative thread. If you have differential feed, use it to prevent stretch.

- Two layers of fabric can be decoratively seamed by flat-locking.

- Casual tops can be finished without facings.

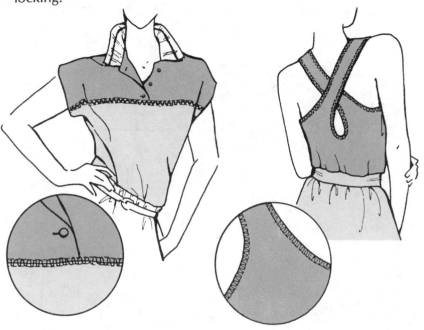

- Reversibles can be made without turning such as this "in minutes" child's jumper.

- Sew aerobic and swimwear in minutes with seams that stretch with the fabric.

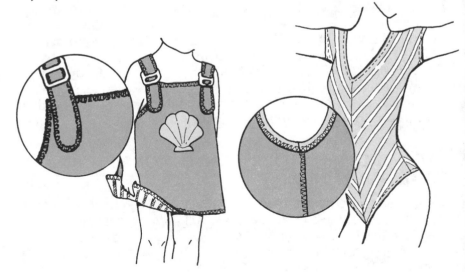

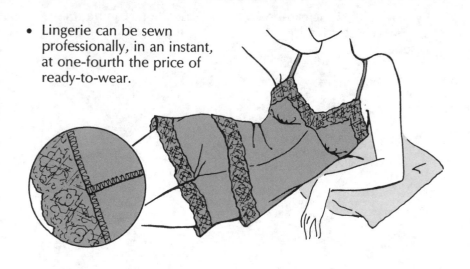

- Lingerie can be sewn professionally, in an instant, at one-fourth the price of ready-to-wear.

Table linens can be beautifully finished with a durable narrow rolled edge.

In this book, we'll show you how to do all that we've illustrated. But what we haven't mentioned is most important — **sergers make sewing FUN!** In fact, serging is so much fun that we are actually SORRY when a garment is finished! It is like MAGIC to watch the ravely edges of a fabric being trimmed . . . in goes the fabric and out comes a beautifully finished seam or edge. We've even seen children so fascinated by the serging process that they stopped watching their computer screens and took up sewing.

YOU STILL NEED YOUR CONVENTIONAL SEWING MACHINE!

Even though there are some garments that can be sewn **entirely** on the serger, most of the time you will use a combination of your conventional machine and your serger. They make a perfect pair. Think of it this way . . . did you toss your knives when you bought your food processor?

10

8 WAYS SERGERS DIFFER FROM CONVENTIONAL SEWING MACHINES

1. **Sergers have "cutters"** (knife blades) that trim the seam allowance before it is overcast.

2. **Serging is a knitting process.** Each stitch is knitted using needles and loopers over a prong or "stitch finger." This metal prong actually stays between the fabric and thread until the stitch is entirely formed. For this reason, the fabric will never draw up or pucker, even when finishing the edge of a lightweight fabric.

stitch finger

looper threads

needle thread

knife

3. **There are no bobbins.** Loopers take the place of bobbins.

4. **Sergers can use 2 or more spools of thread at one time.**

5. **You cannot sew a traditional straight "lockstitch" on a serger** like you can on your conventional machine. However, some sergers can sew a 2-thread "chainstitch" that looks like a straight stitch on the right side. It is slightly bulkier in a seam than a lockstitch.

6. **Sergers feed 2 layers of fabric perfectly!** You can even match stripes without basting as long as you begin with them matched!

7. **Lifting the presser foot is not necessary** when starting to sew unless your fabric is thick. Serger feed dogs are longer than those on a conventional machine and they catch the fabric as it is placed just under the toe of the presser foot.

8. **Sergers won't jam if you sew without fabric** in the machine. Just hold the thread tail or chain lightly behind the presser foot.

Sergers have been used by ready-to-wear manufacturers since the early 1900s. In the 1940's, the Baby Lock was developed as the first serger for home use. While its industrial cousin might sew at 6,000 stitches per minute, the home model was made to sew more slowly and to be lighter in weight, more affordable, and safer to use with a protective cover for the knife blade. Today, nearly every sewing machine manufacturer and some retail fabric chains distribute sergers for home use.

CHAPTER 2

DECISIONS...DECISIONS...WHICH ONE TO BUY?

Having tested more than 15 different sergers while researching for this book, we can say with confidence that each offered unique advantages. Our job is to know many, but we envy you in getting to know **one** single machine well. It is a lot easier than trying to memorize 15 instruction manuals!

BEFORE YOU GO SHOPPING

Read this chapter. As you read about all the features available on a serger, determine which are most and least important to your sewing. Serger features are changing so fast that new features probably will come out as soon as this book is printed. Still, we know you will benefit from our thousands of hours of research when trying to sort out the many machines available today.

UNDERSTANDING STITCHES = UNDERSTANDING SERGERS

Manufacturers offer sergers that can use two, three, four or five threads at one time. For greater versatility, most newer models are convertible to sew more than one stitch type.

If you understand how the stitches are formed and what they do **before** you go shopping, you will be better able to select the serger best suited to your sewing needs. See the chart on pages 14 and 15.

> **NOTE:** To help you understand at a glance how the stitches are formed, use a different color thread for each needle and looper. Better yet, if your machine is color-coded, match the thread to the color codes on the thread guides.

THE SERGER...ITS PARTS

Understanding the functions of the parts of a serger will help you understand how it works. We have illustrated a 3/4-thread machine on page 13 because it is the most common type. A 3-thread machine would have one less needle and one less tension dial, while a 5-thread model would have one more looper and tension dial.

OUR "GENERIC" SERGER

NOTE: The parts illustrated are common to all sergers even though our drawing doesn't resemble any particular serger.

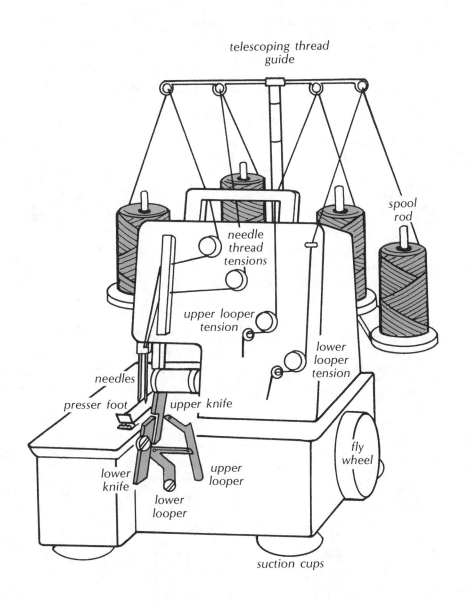

telescoping thread guide

spool rod

needle thread tensions

upper looper tension

lower looper tension

needles

presser foot

upper knife

fly wheel

lower knife

upper looper

lower looper

suction cups

HOW ARE STITCHES FORMED ON SERGERS?

The Stitch and Stitch Formation

2-Thread Overedge—formed in one of two ways:

THE OVER/UNDER METHOD: The upper looper goes over the top of the fabric leaving a loop of thread that is caught by the needle. Then the upper looper goes under the fabric, picks up the needle thread and pulls it to the edge of the fabric. This method is found on "true" 4-thread machines that do a chain stitch.

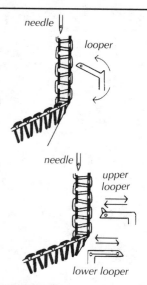

THE PLAY CATCH METHOD: You unthread and plug the upper looper, turning it into a "V"-shaped "hook." The lower looper goes under the fabric and hands a loop of thread to the upper looper which then places it on top of the fabric ready to be caught by the needle. This method is used on machines that do 3-thread stitches where the upper looper goes back and forth over the top of the fabric only and cannot go over AND under the fabric.

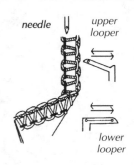

3-Thread Overlock—The threads connect or "lock at the seam line, and the stitch looks approximately the same on both sides.

The upper looper goes *over* the top of the fabric leaving a loop which is caught by the needle.

The lower looper goes *under* the fabric placing a loop of thread under the needle loop then goes out to the edge where it knits together with the upper looper thread.

3/4-Thread Overlock—a 3-thread stitch with an extra needle thread running down the middle. Two types are available. In **A** leave out left or right needle for a narrow or wide 3-thread stitch. In **B** leave out the left needle for a narrow 3-thread stitch. You *must* use both needles if you want a wide stitch.

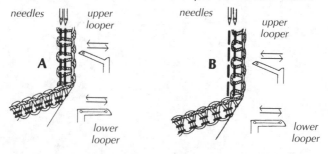

- Called an "overedge" stitch because the threads do not connect or "lock" at the seamline; therefore, it is not used to sew seams.
- Perfect if you primarily want to finish seam allowances and edges.
- With only two threads, seam and edge finishes are less bulky—nice for lightweight fabrics or when using heavier decorative threads.
- Flatlocking is easy and very flat with a 2-thread stitch (see page 66).
- Some 2-thread machines can be adjusted to sew a rolled edge.

- Called an "overlock stitch because the threads connect or "lock" at the seamline. Can be used to sew seams.
- Produces a balanced stitch that looks similar on both sides...great for reversibles.
- With three threads, seam and edge finishes can be slightly bulkier than with two threads because of the additional thread.
- Has lots of give, so is excellent for knits.
- 3-thread machines can flatlock (see page 66).
- Can be adjusted to sew a rolled edge (see page 41)
- Ideal for decorative serging, especially if stitch width goes to 5 or 7 mm.

NOTE: Some 3-thread machines can convert to two threads. Check your manual.

- A 3-thread overlock with the addition of an extra stitch down the middle for added durability.
- All 4 threads are **not** necessary for a serged seam.
- Excellent for clothes that get hard wear and/or frequent washings, like sportswear, childrenswear and menswear.
- Has as much give as a 3-thread stitch.
- Interesting decorative effects created when different color threads are used in the needles and loopers.
- 3/4-thread machines can flatlock by dropping one needle.

NOTE: Several manufacturers are now introducing 3/4-thread machines that can also sew a 3-thread as well as a 2-thread stitch. We call them 2/3/4-thread machines.

True 4-Thread—A chain combined with a 2-thread overedge.

The chain—the left needle and the lower looper form a 2-thread chain stitch.

The 2-thread overedge—the right needle and the upper looper form the 2-thread overedge stitch described on page 14.

All **4** threads are needed to sew a serged **seam**.

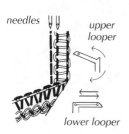

5-Thread Stitch—A chain combined with a 3-thread overlock:

The chain—the left needle and left lower looper form a 2-thread chain stitch.

The 3-thread overlock—formed as described on page 14.

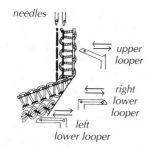

Conversion option: The 3-thread overlock on many 5-thread machines can be converted to a 2-thread overedge. It LOOKS LIKE a "true" 4-thread stitch, but is formed differently.

The chain—formed as described above.

The 2-thread overedge—formed using the play catch method described on page 14.

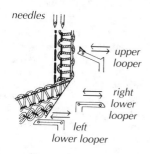

- Made up of a 2-thread chainstitch and a 2-thread overedge stitch. All four threads are necessary to sew a serged seam.
- Well-suited for ravelly, loosely woven fabrics because the chain forms a strong seam and the seam allowance is wider.
- The seam is also wide enough to press flat and even top-stitch.
- It has less stretch than a 3-thread stitch so can stabilize stretchy areas.
- Used whenever a wider seam allowance is desirable for strength (upholstery) or when seam needs to be pressed flat (jackets, slacks).
- Some 4/2-thread machines can sew a rolled edge.

Note: Dropping the left needle leaves a 2-thread overedge stitch for professional finishing of seam allowances and flatlocking. Dropping the right needle leaves the straight chain stitch.

- Sews a 2-thread chain stitch in combination with a 2-thread overedge or a 3-thread overlock stitch.
- Chain stitch, 2-thread overedge, or 3-thread overlock can each be used independently.
- By using the 2-thread chain stitch **and** 3-thread overlock stitch together, the seam is sewn twice for added durability.
- Use the 3-thread overlock stitch alone for seams that require stretch.
- Can sew rolled edges with either 2-thread or 3-thread stitch.
- A very wide 9mm seam width created on some machines when the chain is sewn with either the 2- or 3-thread stitch. Great for durability!!

UNDERSTANDING FEATURES BEFORE YOU SHOP

There are some features that are standard to all sergers. However, they vary depending on the manufacturer. This concise overview will help clarify the variations **before** you go shopping.

STANDARD FEATURES	MANUFACTURERS' VARIATIONS
STITCH LENGTH REGULATOR (or "feed" regulator) LONG SHORT Range: 0-5mm	• **Loosen a screw** or push a button under machine, then • **Turn a** or • **Move a dial** **lever**
STITCH WIDTH REGULATOR WIDE NARROW Range: 1-7mm	• **Move the lower knife** and sometimes the stitch finger by turning a dial or by loosening a screw. • **Change to a throat plate** with a narrower stitch forming finger. • **Remove a needle** Narrower: remove left needle Wider: remove right needle

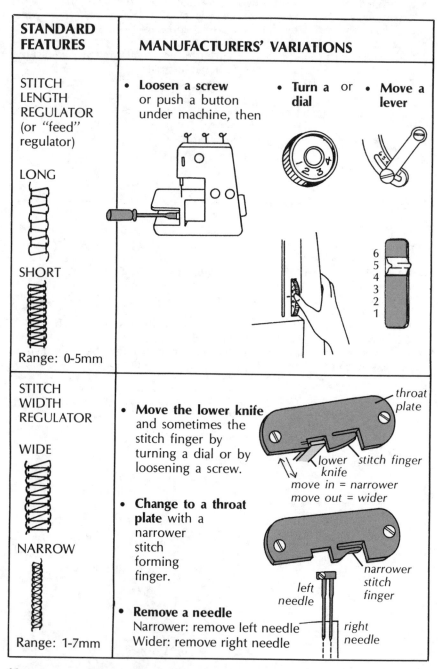

move in = narrower
move out = wider

throat plate

lower knife   stitch finger

narrower stitch finger

left needle   right needle

18

STANDARD FEATURES CONT.	MANUFACTURERS' VARIATIONS
TENSION REGULATOR	Tension dials are either on the outside or set into the machine. The dials turn from one up to ten rotations to loosen or tighten. Turn them right to tighten or left to loosen. (When built in, up loosens and down tightens.) *tighten* *loosen* *loosen* *tighten* Most are either numbered or color-coded to help you easily gauge tension. We avoid adjusting tension on our conventional machines, yet on a serger, it is actually FUN!! Small tension adjustments can entirely change the character of a stitch. Experiment when you are sewing with decorative threads!
PRESSURE REGULATOR	Most sergers have a screw on top of the machine to adjust presser foot pressure. As with tension dials, turn the screw right to tighten or increase pressure and left to loosen or decrease pressure. Increasing pressure, particularly when serging heavy fabrics, can help prevent skipped stitches. Reducing pressure can help prevent stretching in knits.
SAFETY	Home sergers have a knife blade guard or "finger protector," and some have needle guards.
STITCH FINGER	The metal prong that stays between the fabric and the thread until the stitch is entirely formed. Its width determines the stitch width. Can be on the throat plate or presser foot. (See page 18.)

STANDARD FEATURES	MANUFACTURERS' VARIATIONS
NEEDLES *front* *back* *groove (always to the front)* *scarf (always to the back)*	**Conventional or household (15X1) needles** (used on some sergers)—They come in a wide range of sizes (9-18) and are easy to find. The shank is flat on the side that's inserted to the back, it's easy to guide the needle into the proper position. **Industrial needles (DC X 1, DC X 1F, BL X 1, DB X 1, JL X1)**—Industrial needles are available in sizes 9-16. They are specifically designed to be long-lasting for high-speed sewing. With the exception of the DC X 1F, they have a round shank. **Custom needles**—are adaptions made specifically for a certain brand or model. A ball point needle may be necessary when serging nylon/spandex fabric. Sew a test seam and pull on it. If you see holes, use a ball point needle.
FLY WHEEL	The trend is for serger fly wheels to rotate counter-clockwise, the same as most conventional machines, but some models rotate clockwise. Determine which is the proper rotation for your machine, and **mark the direction with an arrow on masking tape**.
PRESSER FOOT LEVER	Most sergers have the lever at the back on the left side, but a few manufacturers have moved the presser foot lever to the right side of the machine.
EASY THREADING	For easier threading, companies have added color coding to their thread guides, tension knobs, and loopers as well as a color-coded chart painted on the machine.
KNIFE BLADES	There is usually an upper and a lower knife blade. Depending on the machine, one is made of a hard carbide steel and the other of a softer steel. The lower blade is stationary, the upper blade moves. The blades can be disengaged on some machines when trimming is not desired.

OPTIONAL FEATURES	MANUFACTURERS' VARIATIONS
BUILT-IN LIGHT	Lighting is important. Depending on where the light is built into the machine, it may or may not be adequate. You may still prefer auxiliary lights.
ROLLED EDGE ATTACHMENT	Some sergers require a special plate and/or foot in order to sew a rolled edge. Others can be adjusted for roll hemming without an attachment.
BUILT-IN ACCESSORY BOX	Built-in storage for tweezers, screwdriver, etc. A handy feature for serger owners with small children or space limitations.
MATERIAL WASTE CONTAINER	An accessory that fits below the serger knives to catch the trimmings. If your machine doesn't have one, you can purchase a trim catcher separately. Or, simply tape a paper lunch bag to the sewing table. YOU WILL NEED IT!
SPECIAL FEET	To help you more easily handle specific serging tasks, many manufacturers offer several special presser feet. The **blind hem foot**, for example, is often a standard accessory. Options may include an **elastic applicator foot** (or "elasticator") that automatically stretches elastic as it is being serged onto the garment (also can apply narrow ribbons and tapes); a **tape sewing foot** with a slot through which twill or other narrow tapes and ribbons (or narrow elastic) can be fed while serging; a **beading foot** for application of strings of beads, sequins, or pearls (also useful to apply filler cords or other cording); and a **piping foot** for creating piping with a seam allowance.
DIFFERENTIAL FEED	Prevents puckers as well as stretching and assists in gathering. See page 123 for how it works. Also see pages 8, 49, 53, 73, 103.

NOW GO SHOPPING!

Take this book for handy reference and 3"×10" swatches of fabrics you frequently sew (preferably knits **and** wovens, heavy to light weight). After the dealer demonstration, ask if you can serge your fabrics. Try all the features on the machine including the attachments.

All About Thread
AND EASIEST THREADING

CHAPTER 3

ALL ABOUT THREAD AND EASIEST THREADING

A lot of thread is used in a serged seam or edge finish. But don't be tempted to buy poor quality thread to save money. It can only cause you headaches! We test most serger threads and discuss thread preferences with serger manufacturers, so we can make you be a savvy thread shopper. PLUS, we think you'll find threading your serger is **easy** if you follow the tips in this chapter.

HOW MUCH THREAD DO YOU NEED?

Have you found storing all those cones a problem? You rarely need 3,000 yards that you will find on some cones. In fact, 250 meter spools will be more than enough to serge most garments. Storage will be easier, the color range much larger, and the cost less. The needle uses the least amount of thread and is the only thread that "could" show as it is the only one penetrating the fabric. You should match your needle thread, but could use "blending" colors in the loopers.

FIVE CHARACTERISTICS OF SERGER THREAD

You'll find special serger threads in fabric and sewing machine stores. The following characteristics of serger thread make it ideal for high-speed sewing:

1. **Size** — Because so many threads are used in serged seams and seam finishes, serger thread is slightly finer in size than conventional all-purpose thread.

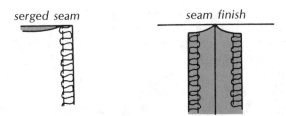

serged seam   seam finish

2. **Strength** — Because of serger speed (1300 to 1700 stitches per minute) and the number of guides the thread must pass through, the thread is exposed to a great deal of heat from friction as well as abrasion. Therefore, a special finish is applied to serger thread to make it extra smooth for high-speed sewing.

3. **Thread winding** — Some conventional thread is "parallel-wound" or "stacked" on the spool because the first thread guide on most conventional machines is **to the side** of the spool and the spool turns as the thread is used.

The first thread guide on a serger is **directly above** the spool and the spool does not turn during sewing. Thread designed for sergers, therefore, is "cross-wound" so it will reel off the top evenly and easily during high-speed sewing. You can, however, adapt conventional spools for serger use (see page 25). Some conventional spools are cross-wound.

Cross-wound thread for sergers.

Parallel-wound thread for conventional machines.

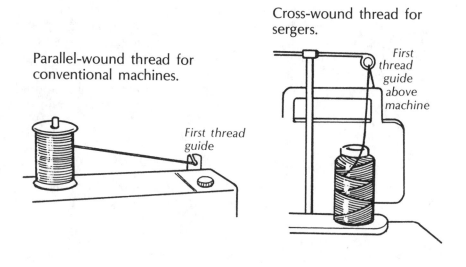

First thread guide above machine

First thread guide

4. **Color** — Coned serger thread comes in fewer colors than conventional thread. It is important to match the needle thread as it is the only thread that goes through the fabric. The looper threads can blend with the fabric. Therefore, you may choose to use conventional thread in the needle. You shouldn't have a problem using different threads in the needles and loopers, but may have to make slight tension adjustments if they vary slightly in size.

5. **Spool type** — Several spool styles are available for use on your serger.

Cone

King Tube

Compact Tube

Cones were developed for clothing manufacturers and hold thousands of yards of thread. You probably won't need 6,000 yards of fuchsia, so consider large cones for basic colors. Smaller yardage cones are also available.

King tubes have less yardage than cones yet have a wide base that helps the thread continue to reel off easily, even when it is running low. King tubes fit over the adapters.

Compact tubes fit on the spool rod without an adaptor. They have more yardage (averaging 1500 yards) than a king tube (1,000 yards), and are stored easily.

NOTE: You can make any spool type work on your serger with the help of the following:

Cone adaptors — Since cones are wider at the base, place an adaptor (supplied with your machine) over the spool rod to hold the cone tight and secure.

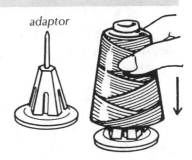

adaptor

Spool caps — Place spool on rod with notched end **down**. Place cap over spool. It is wider than the top of the spool to help the thread reel off freely. Caps are supplied with your machine.

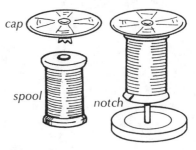

cap

spool

notch

6. **Thread fiber content** —Any fiber content of thread will work in the serger, but each has its advantages and disadvantages. Following are the characteristics of each:

100% polyester has strength, resiliency and good abrasion resistance. Long-staple polyester threads are uniform in thickness.

100% cotton sews well, is more lustrous, dyes well and is available in a wide range of colors, but has more limited elasticity and less strength than polyester.

Cotton-covered polyester sews well like cotton, yet has the strength, uniformity and abrasion resistance of polyester in the core.

Silk is strong and has a high luster, but is relatively expensive and scarce. Its fine size makes it well-suited for lightweight fabrics, and it makes beautiful satin and rolled edge finishes.

Monofilament nylon looks like fine fishing line. It is very strong, somewhat coarse (unless in the fine #80 size), and transparent.

"Woolly" nylon is untwisted and texturized, similar to fine yarn. It can be used to enhance thread coverage of an edge, to yield softer serged seams and edge finishes, and to tighten the lower looper of a rolled edge.

Rayon has a silk-like luster but is less expensive than silk, and is available in a variety of weights. One of our favorites is Decor 6, a heavier, untwisted rayon filament thread.

Metallic thread can be used in the loopers for special effects. You will need to adjust (generally loosen) looper tensions when using this low-resiliency thread. Metallic threads with a polyester core better withstand the rigors of serging. Some metallic threads work better than others. Experiment!

BUY IT THREADED!!

Before you take your serger home, thread it 3 times in the presence of your dealer just to make sure you know how. If you take it home threaded, you may never again have to thread it "from scratch." However, keep your manual handy in case you accidentally unthread the machine.

It could have taken weeks to learn how to thread an industrial serger. Today's home models are so much easier! They even have color coded thread guides and threading charts printed right on the machine for easy reference. You can even use three different colors of thread that **match** your thread guides when learning to use your serger.

THREADING TIPS

Consult your serger manual for the correct threading order. On most sergers, thread the upper looper first, then the lower looper. If you have more than one needle, it doesn't matter which needle you thread first, as long as the needles are **last**. Trickiest to thread is the lower looper; although recent design changes, such as self-threading or two-part loopers and openable housings, have simplified the process.

Make sure threads are in the tension disks. Tug each thread just below the tension dial—you should feel resistance on each thread.

THE EASIEST THREADING METHOD OF ALL!

Check your manual first, as these steps may vary with different models.

1. Clip the threads on the machine just above each spool. Replace spools with different threads.

2. Tie the new threads onto the old. Tug on the knot to make sure it is secure. No need to clip the tails close to the knots.

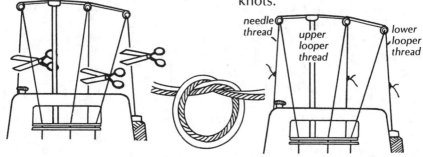

3. Pull needle thread(s) through the guides. Clip the knot before it reaches the eye of the needle. Rethread needle(s).

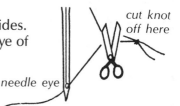

4. Lift presser foot and slowly pull looper threads, **one at a time**, through the machine until the knots pass through and out the back of the machine. (Knots in thicker decorative threads **may** be too large to pull through.)

> **NOTE:** If it is difficult to pull threads through machine, **loosen all the tensions** or just slip the threads out of the tension disks, and raise the presser foot. (On some models, the tensions are released automatically when you lift the foot or touch a release lever.) Readjust tension after threading is completed.

5. Now you are ready to serge. See page 33 for how to create your first thread chain.

> **HINT:** After **rethreading** a broken lower looper thread, make sure the needle thread is on top of the throat plate before you begin to serge again. Otherwise, the lower looper thread will break again.

CHAPTER 4

GET READY TO SEW

Planning ahead is important when using a serger. Your first decision is what type of seam to use ... ¼″ serged seams or ⅝″ seams with serged seam allowances that will be pressed open. Your choice will affect how you transfer pattern markings to your fabric, how you fit, and your sewing order.

Use serged seams:

3.5-7mm

- In most knits where seams must stretch with the garment and where narrow seams are more appropriate for the fabric.
- In woven fabrics where seams will not be strained (loose fitting garments) and where bulk is not a concern.
- In lightweight fabrics that pucker easily.

NOTE: You can't easily serge seams that are outside corners (see page 37).

Use conventional seams and serge the seam allowances:

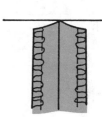

- In medium- to heavy-weight woven fabrics.
- Where seams should be flat and pressed open, as on fitted gabardine trousers.
- Where pockets or zipper are in the seam.
- When you need wider seam allowances to allow for fitting changes.

DON'T JUST SAVE TIME SERGING — CUT FASTER TOO!

My, how sewing has changed! What would our grandmothers think about all the new equipment available today? We not only have sergers, but rotary cutters!

Rotary cutters are round razor blades attached to a handle (like a pizza cutter). The blade turns or rolls along the edge of your pattern, cutting the fabric.

Rotary cutters come in 2 sizes, small and large. We prefer the small one for most cutting as it is easier to control. However, when we cut thick coatings or quilted fabrics, the large one is indispensible!

Use a plastic mat under your fabric so you won't damage your table. Instead of pins, use weights or any small heavy object such as caviar or baby food jars, heavy ashtrays, or cans to hold your fabric in place. Cut with the blade against the edge of the pattern and the screw side to the outside.

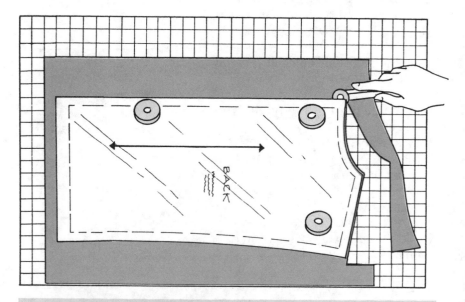

NOTE: Rotary cutters do not replace dressmaking shears. Your first investment should always be quality shears.

PATTERN MARKINGS

Use either notches or snips to align layers of fabric when serging a seam.

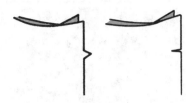

However, if finishing seam allowances **before** seaming, the notches and snips will be trimmed off. Instead, mark notches and dots in the seam allowance, next to the seamline with a water soluble marking pen.

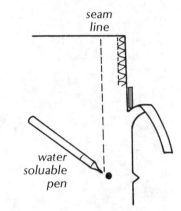

seam line

water soluable pen

FIT FIRST

After you cut-to-fit, it's a good idea to pin-fit the fabric, wrong sides together, with pins along the seam line, parallel to the edge. Then try on the garment. Remember, serged seams are automatically trimmed to a narrow width. The garment cannot be let out and made larger!

Move pins, to take in or let out, until fit is correct. Take off the garment. Open up seam allowances and mark the new seam line with a water soluble marker. Remove pins. Place fabric layers right sides together and serge confidently with the needle on the marked seam line!

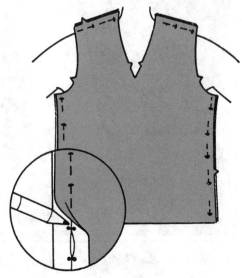

Serge Ahead...
SEWING TIPS

CHAPTER 5

SERGE AHEAD...SEWING TIPS

Sewing has never been so exciting. Serging is like magic! We have even seen little children so fascinated with serging that they begged their mothers to let them take up sewing.

With a little practice, you'll master estimating seam allowance width, plus sewing curves and corners. Sit down at your serger right now and try the following:

GET THE MACHINE READY

You'll need a 4" chain or "tail" of thread behind the presser foot before you begin to serge. To create a chain, do the following:

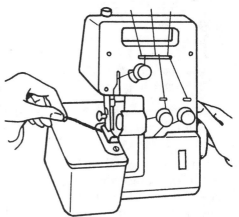

1. Pull the threads to the left under the presser foot, as shown.

2. Lightly hold the threads with your left hand (lowering the presser foot helps). Turn the fly wheel a few times with your right hand. Then lightly step on the foot pedal until a 2" chain of thread is formed.

SEW A TEST SEAM FIRST

Before serging any garment, sew a test seam on scraps. Your fabric should be cut on the same grain as your actual seams. A perfect seam should . . .

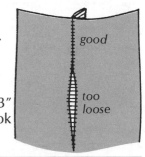

good

too
loose

. . . have balanced tension (see page 50).
. . . stay together when you strain the seam.
. . . not pucker (see page 53).
. . . not stretch the fabric (see page 53).
. . . not be bulky (see page 23).

A perfect test sample is 45" long and 3" wide. Serge...look...adjust...serge...look ...adjust, etc.

NOTE: We tell you how to solve stitching problems in Chapter 7.

HELP! WHERE IS THE SEAM LINE?

Remember, the seam line is where the needle enters the fabric. It is **not** where the knife cuts! If you begin with a ⅝" seam allowance, and your knives cut off ⅜", a ¼" seam allowance will remain.

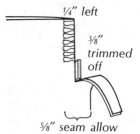

¼" left

⅜" trimmed off

⅝" seam allow

Some sergers have a marked stitching guide on the front of the machine. If your machine has no guide, use one of the following marking methods:

- Use masking tape or pre-marked Tape Stitch Sewing Tape™ on the knife blade cover on the front of the machine.

- Mark the seam line on your fabric with a water soluble or air erasable (disappears without water in 24 hours) marking pen.

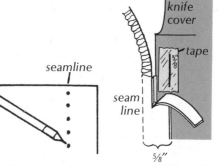

machine knife cover

tape

seamline

seam line

⅝"

After using a serger for awhile, you will soon develop the ability to eyeball or "guesstimate" the accurate seam line by watching what is cut off. Honest!!

But Gail also finds a needle line marking on the front of the serger foot indispensable — that way, she can guide the fabric accurately before it is cut. If a needle line isn't already marked on the foot, mark it with a fine-point, permanent felt-tip pen.

SEW WITHOUT PINS

Pins aren't necessary because the serger feeds the fabric evenly through the machine. You can even match stripes without pins if you begin sewing with the stripes matched!

If you forget to take a pin out and the knife blades hit it, one or both of the blades can be damaged. That can get expensive! Try the following if you are having trouble sewing without pins:

- Pin, but remove pins **before** they hit the knives. Use pins with large heads so they won't get lost in the fabric.

- Pin inside the seam line.

- Hand baste.

- Glue baste the layers together with water soluble glue stick. Lightly dot the glue on the one seam allowance every 2 to 3". Then stick the two seam allowances right sides together. Dots can be closer when using slippery fabrics or as a guarantee for matching stripes!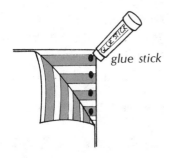

glue stick

NOTE: Pati was serging a wonderful rayon faille that wiggled so much she couldn't control the fabric. She could have used water soluble glue stick, but part of the garment was bias so rubbing glue on the edges stretched them. She was forced into hand basting, but decided it was faster than ripping out a serged seam.

NOW SEW STRAIGHT SEAMS

1. It is not necessary to raise the presser foot with most fabrics. Insert fabric under the toe of the foot. The longer feed dogs will automatically grab the fabric and pull it under the foot.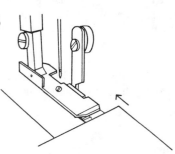

NOTE: With some slippery or heavy fabrics, you will need to lift the presser foot and slide the fabric under it up to the knives. Lower the presser foot and begin to sew.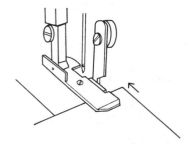

2. Hold the chain lightly and gently press the foot pedal. Start sewing slowly at first, with your hands guiding the fabric and controlling the amount being cut off.

NOW SEW CURVED SEAMS

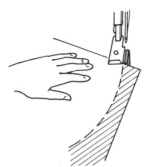

For inside or outside curves, the trick is watching the seam allowance where the knife is cutting rather than at the needle as you would with a conventional machine. Otherwise guide the fabric as you would if straight stitching.

Practice makes perfect. Curves were difficult for us at first, but now they seem easy. When the seams are quite curved, lift the presser foot every few inches and turn the fabric under it.

NOW SEW CORNERED SEAMS

Inside corners — Inside cornered seams, such as when facing a square neckline, can be serged. They turn quite well without even clipping the threads at the corner (which you wouldn't want to do or your seam would rip out). Serge a TEST SAMPLE to make sure you like the results.

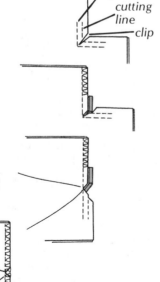

1. Mark stitching and cutting lines within 1" of the corner using a washable marker. Clip to the corner.

2. Stitch seam until knife comes to cutting line on next edge.

3. Straighten the corner. You will have a "V" fold of fabric at the corner. Don't worry, the pleat will disappear after serging.

4. Serge remaining edge.

5. The inside cornered seam is finished. **Do not clip corner**. Turn and press.

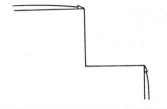

NOTE: If your test sample indicates the corner should have been reinforced before serging with short straight stitches, simply sew the entire seam on your straight stitch machine. No sense stitching and serging when one will do!

Outside Corners—Do not sew outside cornered seams on your serger. When you trim and slash corners before turning you would cut your stitches, causing them to rip out. For example, **you can't serge collars right sides together** and turn. Use a conventional machine instead. Corners will be less bulky.

CHAIN OFF AT THE END OF A SEAM

1. At the end of a seam, keep sewing until you have a 5" thread chain. This is called "chaining off."

2. Cut the chain leaving 3" on the machine and 2" on the fabric.

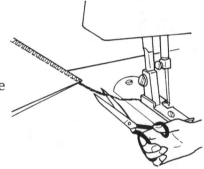

CUT THE CHAIN WITHOUT SCISSORS

An **easy** way to cut threads at the end of a seam is to let the knives do it. Bring the fabric to the front of the machine with the chain over or under the presser foot.

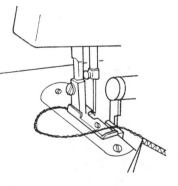

SECURE THE END OF A SEAM

You can't backstitch on a serger! The loose loops at the beginning or end of a seam can come undone and the seam can ravel out. Use one of the following methods to secure the stitching:

- **Tie a knot** and put a dab of seam sealant such as Fray Check™ or Fray-No-More™ on it. After it dries, cut off the chain. (Use rubbing alcohol to remove any unwanted sealant.)

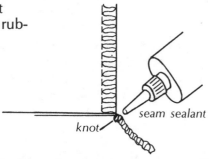

seam sealant

knot

- **Bury the chain** by threading it through a large tapestry needle (they have a blunt point) and running it under the last few stitches.

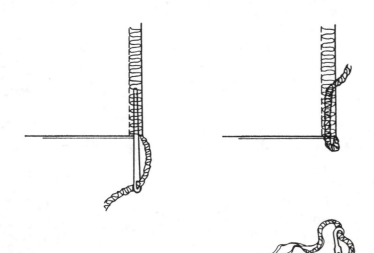

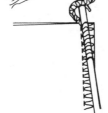

OR, use that loop turner that's sitting in your drawer. The moveable latch opens as you move down the stitches and closes when you come back up with the chain.

- **Use your machine to secure a seam!**
  - At the **beginning** of a seam.

When the needle has made one stitch into edge of fabric, lift presser foot and swing chain to front.

Place chain on seam allowance. Lower presser foot.

Stitch over chain.

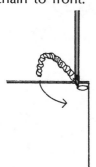

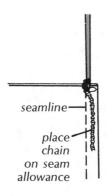

seamline

place
chain
on seam
allowance

— At the **end** of a seam stop sewing when the needle is one stitch off the fabric.

Gently slip chain off stitch finger (pulling a slight amount of slack above needle will make this easier—see page 47). Raise presser foot. Flip fabric over and to front of the machine.

Lower presser foot and stitch **over** last few stitches. Be careful not to cut the stitches already sewn. Chain off and trim the chain.

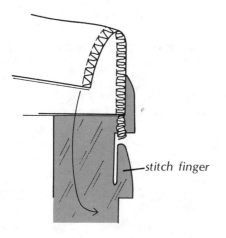

stitch finger

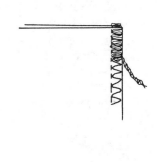

RIPPING SERGING IS EASY

For 3- and 3/4-thread stitches

Pull on the needle thread(s). If necessary, work in short segments. When it comes out completely, the looper threads fall off.

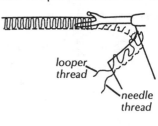

As an alternative, slip a small seam ripper under the loops on one side, cutting them. The needle and looper threads on the other side will easily pull out.

looper thread

needle thread

For 2-thread overedge

Pull on needle and looper threads equally and at the same time. They will pull out easily.

For 2-thread chainstitch

Clip needle thread; pull on looper thread. It instantly comes out!

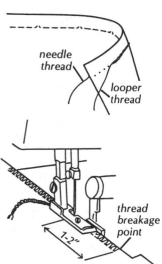

needle thread

looper thread

WHEN THREADS BREAK DURING SEWING

1. Check the threading. Have any threads come out of the thread guides?

2. Form a new chain 2 inches long.

3. Place needle in seam line with the knife blades against the edge, overlapping previous stitches about 1-2″ from where the thread broke.

thread breakage point

1-2″

4. Start serging, being careful not to cut original stitches with knife.

STABILIZING SEAMS

In **stress areas** of fitted garments, such as the crotch of pants, you may need extra strength. This is especially important in loosely woven or knitted fabrics.

Also, stretching at shoulder seams, neckline and front edges can be a problem in knits. To stabilize any seam, try one of the following:

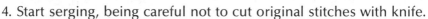

Sew a row of straight stitching inside the serged seam.	Serge over ¼″ twill tape.	Serge over yarn or buttonhole twist.

Professional Finishing

WITH A SERGER

CHAPTER 6

PROFESSIONAL FINISHING WITH A SERGER

One of the most exciting uses for a serger is beautiful finishing of seam allowances and edges. The serger sews clean, flat and pucker-free, even on single layers. This chapter covers the basics using regular threads. Chapter 8 takes these finishing ideas one step further with heavier decorative threads.

FINISHING SEAM ALLOWANCES

When you sew a regular seam on a conventional machine and press it open, the seam allowances will need to be finished if the fabric is ravely.

The best seam finish is one that is not bulky. A 2-thread stitch is the most delicate, but a 3-thread is suitable in most cases. A 3/4-thread stitch is ideal for extremely ravely fabrics because the extra stitch adds strength.

A medium to wide stitch width and a medium to long stitch length will reduce thread density and be less bulky. Always SEW A TEST SAMPLE on a scrap of fabric to make sure you like the seam finish.

Finish the seam allowance before sewing to prevent raveling during garment construction. Finishing also puts you in a mood to sew. When the garment is finished, so is the finishing!

However, allow the knives to only **skim** the edge of the fabric and not cut off part of the seam allowance. In an unlined jacket, you would finish the following edges first:

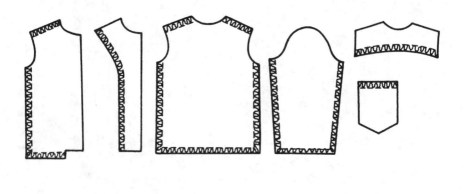

FINISHING EDGES

Finishing outside edges is somewhat decorative even with matching thread. Use rayon or silk thread for added shine or Woolly Nylon for better coverage. See Chapter 8 for more thread ideas.

Two popular edge finishes are the narrow edge and the narrow rolled edge. Actually, the fabric in both rolls under because the distance between the knives and the stitch finger is greater than the width of the stitch. They **differ in tension** adjustments.

Narrow (unrolled) edge

This finish is sewn with a narrow (2mm) 2- or 3-thread **balanced** stitch. The upper and lower threads meet at the edge. A narrow edge is quite flat compared to a narrow **rolled** edge because the fabric rolls less.

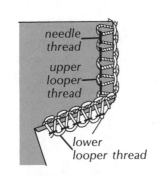

Narrow rolled edge

A narrow rolled edge can be sewn on most models with a 2-thread overedge or a 3-thread overlock stitch. The tension is **unbalanced** and the stitch width 2mm or less. The upper looper thread in a 3-thread stitch and the looper thread in a 2-thread stitch are pulled all the way over the edge of the fabric, encasing it. This requires considerable tightening of the needle thread tension in a 2-thread stitch and the lower looper tension in a 3-thread stitch.

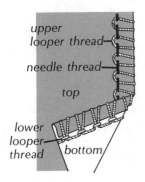

Shorten the stitch length until the stitches are close if a satin edge is desired. Long stitches will create a picot or scalloped edge. A narrow rolled edge is a very durable finish that can stand up to frequent launderings, especially when a short stitch length is used. However, the stitches can be pulled out on the crosswise grain of a loosely woven fabric. If this happens, try lengthening the stitches. Always make a TEST SAMPLE!

Various serger manufacturers also call a narrow rolled edge by other names in their manuals including...

...narrow rolled hem　　...lapping stitch
...felling stitch　　...curling stitch
...handkerchief hem　　...folding stitch
...roll-over stitch

Before making tension adjustments for a rolled edge, read your manual for exact instructions. You will usually need to do the following: (A 3-thread stitch is used in our example.)

1. Place the fabric on the throat plate right side up—the fabric rolls under. An exception is tricot which automatically rolls to the right side. Why fight it? Place tricot right side down.

2. Tighten the lower looper tension a lot. The upper looper thread will then be pulled to the under side, rolling the edge of the fabric under. You may also need to loosen the upper looper a little to help the edge roll.

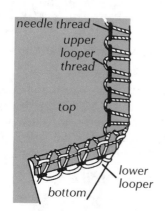

3. If the needle thread loosens under the strain as shown, tighten the needle tension. If it is **too tight**, however, the edge may pucker.

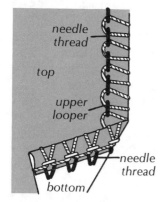

4. Here is a **perfect rolled edge**. The upper looper has been pulled **all the way** to the under side. The needle and lower looper threads appear to be one.

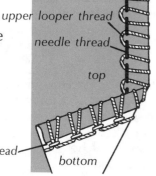

STITCHING IN A CIRCLE

There are 2 ways to stitch in a circle. The first is great for edge of turned up hem, but would look untidy on an exposed edge like a neckline or a placemat. Use the second method for those items.

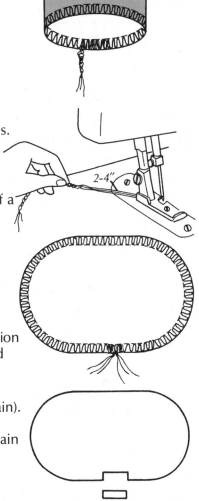

Method I

Stitch 2" over the beginning stitches. Chain off the edge. Tie a knot near edge of fabric. Seal the knot with seam sealant (page 38). When knot is dry, cut off chain.

Method II

1. To pull out unchained threads remove threads from tension dials. You may need to turn the handwheel once.

2. Place threads back into tension disks. **Beginning in the middle** of a straight edge, serge around the edge, not trimming off seam allowance.

3. When knife comes to beginning stitches, raise upper knife. Serge two stitches over beginning stitches.

4. Again, remove threads from tension dials and pull out a 4" unchained tail.

5. Tie knots in each tail (less bulky than if you tied a knot in the chain). Weave threads into serging on under side. Seal knot and cut chain as in Method I

NOTE: Use the above technique even if you have a seam allowance. Simply cut away a 2" section of the seam allowance where you plan to begin and end stitching. Proceed as above, trimming the seam allowance as you serge.

TURNING INSIDE CORNERS

Inside corners are actually easier to finish than outside corners. Use the following technique:

1. Mark the cutting line within 1" of both sides of corner using a washable marker.

2. Clip to corner.

NOTE: If the edge being finished has no seam allowance, it is unnecessary to mark or clip. Simply straighten the edge and stitch as in step 4.

3. Stitch until the front of **knife** comes to corner.

4. Straighten the corner. You will have a "V" fold of fabric at the corner. Don't worry, the pleat will disappear after serging.

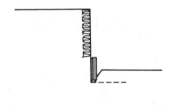

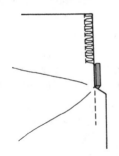

5. Stitch the straightened edge.

6. Now the inside corner is finished!

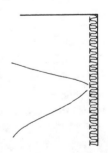

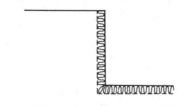

TURNING OUTSIDE CORNERS

The easiest way to finish an outside corner is to turn it into a curve! But, when a **corner** is necessary, there are two ways to handle it. Practice these techniques on scraps until you MASTER them. An hour or two experimenting now will save many hours later when serging a garment. Use one of these methods:

Chain off the edge. On each new edge, stitch over previous stitching. At every corner, chain off. Then either tie a knot and bury the tail or dab the corner with seam sealant and cut off the tail (see page 37). Make a TEST sample to see if you like the results.

Turn the corner. This method is also easy, but requires some practice on scraps . . . so be patient! Follow these steps:

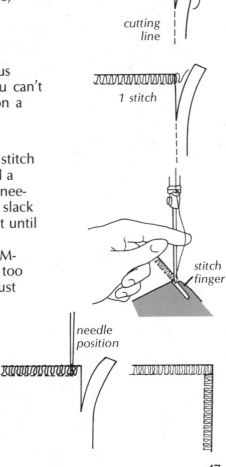

1. Trim along cutting line for 2". If you have no seam allowance, follow steps 2 through 4.

2. Stitch up to the cut edge plus ONE stitch. Raise needle (you can't pivot with needle in fabric on a serger).

3. Gently pull the chain off the stitch finger (To make this easy, pull a **small** amount of slack in the needle thread. Pulling too much slack will create a loop. Experiment until you determine just the right amount. REMEMBER TEST SAMPLES! If you accidentally pull too much, pull the thread back just above the tension dial.)

4. Pivot the fabric. Lower the needle near top edge the same distance in from the unfinished edge as previous stitching. **Then** lower the presser foot.

Perfect Serging
ON ANY FABRIC

CHAPTER 7

PERFECT SERGING ON ANY FABRIC

If you start with a clean, well oiled and properly threaded serger, stitching problems should be minimal. However, the following machine adjustments may be necessary to serge perfectly on any fabric (see pages 18-19, 50-52 for methods of adjustment).

1. **Stitch length**—The longer the stitch length, the more likely a seam is to separate or pull apart, especially on lightweight or loosely woven fabrics. However, a longer stitch means less thread in the seam and therefore a less bulky seam. A rule of thumb is longer stitch length on heavier fabrics and shorter stitch length on lighter fabrics.

2. **Stitch width**—A guideline is to use a wider stitch width on heavier fabrics, narrower on lighter weight fabrics. A wide stitch can sometimes cause puckering on lightweight fabrics. On the other hand, a wide stitch will be more durable on extremely ravely fabrics.

3. **Presser foot pressure**—The pressure rarely needs adjusting. You may wish to decrease it to prevent puckering of lightweight fabrics or stretching of knits. You may need to increase it for heavier fabrics to feed properly and prevent skipped stitches. Very thick napped fabrics, such as fake fur, however, may require less presser foot pressure.

4. **Tension**—The flow of thread from the spool to fabric is controlled by tension dials. Most machines require little tension adjustment for regular serging. The needle thread tension, though, may need adjustment when going from very lightweight to heavy fabrics. Make a test seam. If seam pulls apart, tighten the needle tension. If seam puckers, loosen tension. Tension dials generally need to be adjusted for decorative serging.

5. **Needle size**—The thread and the fabric determine the appropriate needle size. The larger the thread, the larger the needle must be. A too-large needle, however, can damage lightweight or delicate-surfaced fabrics.

6. **Differential feed**—The two sets of feed dogs can move at the same or differing rates. The lower setting prevents puckers. The higher setting prevents stretch in knits and can be used to gather.

A GUIDE TO BALANCED TENSION FOR ANY SERGER

For seaming, you will primarily use a balanced tension. To learn about tension, begin with all tension dials turned to a midpoint. Use a different color thread in each looper and needle. Take a **long** strip of fabric and sew for 3-4". One at a time, turn each dial tighter, then looser. Watch to see what happens to the needle and looper threads. The following tips will show you how to achieve balanced tension with any stitch.

> **NOTE:** The term "upper" looper refers to the thread lying on **top** of the fabric. The lower looper is the thread lying on the **under** side of the fabric. The 2-thread overedge stitch uses only one looper, so we simply call it the "looper" thread. The needle thread can be seen on the top **and** underside of the fabric.

> **RULE OF THUMB NOTE:** Only adjust one dial at a time and ALWAYS loosen the one that is too tight first.

Balanced tension in a 2-thread overedge stitch:

The looper and needle threads interlock at the edge of the fabric.

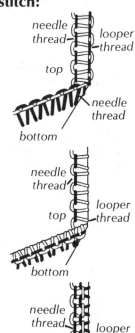

2-thread tension problems look like this:

Problem:
- The looper thread wraps to the under side of the fabric.

Solution:
- Either loosen the needle tension or tighten the looper tension.

Problem:
- The needle thread wraps to the top side of the fabric.

Solution:
- Either tighten the needle tension or loosen the looper tension.

Balanced tension in a 3-thread stitch:

The upper and lower looper threads interlock at the edge of the fabric. The needle thread looks like a straight stitch on the top side and appears only as dots of thread on the under side.

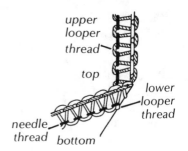

3-thread tension problems look like this:

Problem:
- The needle thread loops on the under side of the fabric.

Solution:
- Generally, tighten the needle tension and test. Sometimes, loosen the lower and/or upper looper tensions.

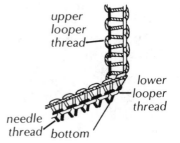

Problem:
- The upper looper thread is pulled to the under side.

Solution:
- Loosen the lower looper tension first and test. Possibly you'll need to tighten the upper looper tension.

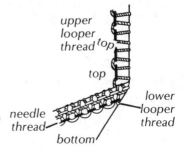

Problem:
- The lower looper thread is pulled to the top side of the fabric.

Solution:
- Loosen the upper looper tension and test. Possibly you'll need to tighten the lower looper tension.

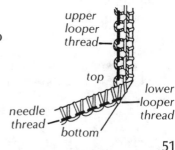

51

Balanced tension in a 3/4-thread stitch:

The upper and lower looper threads interlock at the fabric edge. The needle threads look like straight stitches on the top side and appear only as dots of thread on the under side.

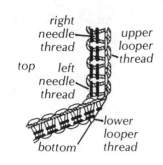

Tension problems look like this:

A 3/4-thread stitch is adjusted as a 3-thread stitch (see page 51). And if the right needle tension is too loose, it will look like this. You need to tighten **only that** tension dial.

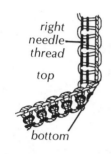

Balanced tension in a 4-thread stitch:

The looper and the right needle threads interlock at the fabric edge. The chainstitch is flat and snug to the fabric.

NOTE: To solve problems with the 2-thread overedge stitch, see page 52.

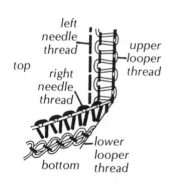

2-thread chainstitch tension problems look like this:

Problem:
- The needle thread "arcs" on the under side of the fabric.

Solution:
- Tighten the left needle and/or loosen the lower looper.

NOTE: For problems and solutions for the 5-thread stitch, see individual sections for the 2-thread chainstitch, the 2-thread overedge and 3-thread overlock.

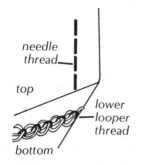

TROUBLE-FREE SERGING

The following solutions will help you serge trouble-free, no matter what type or weight fabric is used:

Problem	Solutions
• **Skipped stitches**	• Replace a bent, dull or damaged needle. • Thread correctly, through all guides and eyes. (Thread can easily come out of the open thread guides.) • Change needle size. • Insert needle correctly. • Increase pressure for heavier fabrics.
• **Puckered fabric**	• Loosen thread tension (lightweight fabrics). • Lighten foot pressure (lightweight fabrics). • Shorten stitch length. • Use differential feed set at .5.
• **Excessive stretching**	• Lighten foot pressure. • Lengthen stitch. • Stabilize edge with interfacing, facings, or by serging over cording or ribbon. • Serge in from the edge, trimming off at least ¼″. • Use differential feed set at 2.
• **Irregular stitches**	• Adjust tensions. • Thread correctly. • Replace with a new or different size needle. • Check needle position. • Change to the correct size needle for thread or fabric.
• **Fabric doesn't feed well**	• Lengthen stitch. • Increase or decrease foot pressure depending on fabric. • Clean lint out of feed dog.
• **Thread is breaking**	• Checking for thread out of guides or for tangling. • Loosen tension. • Release thread if caught in spool notch. • Insert needle correctly. • Change to a new, or a different size needle.
• **Needle breaks**	• Change to a new needle. • Insert the needle correctly. • Change to a larger needle. • Avoid excessive pulling of fabric while serging.
• **Machine jams**	• Pull thread tails to the back as you begin to serge. • Make sure fabric trimmings fall away from, not into, serger. • Lengthen stitch, especially if using heavy threads. • Close protective front cover while serging. • Serge fewer layers of fabric.

Problem	Solutions
• **Trimmed edge is ragged**	• Reset knife blades correctly. • Change to a new blade.
• **Machine sews loudly**	• Oil and clean machine. • Change to a new, correct size needle for fabric or thread. • Consult your dealer if problem persists.

LOVE AND CARE OF YOUR SERGER

Home-use sergers are sturdy machines and quite trouble-free if properly maintained. Most serging problems can be prevented if you do the following:

• Keep it clean

Lint will quickly build up under the throat plate and clog knife blades, causing skipped stitches. Dust out the machine often with a soft brush (one is supplied with your machine) or use non-aerosol compressed air (available at fabric, sewing machine and camera stores). Attach the long narrow tube to the can's nozzle for the most powerful spray. Use sparingly.

• Oil as necessary

Some sergers require no oiling, so consult your manual or dealer for where and how often to oil your model. Oil lightly—usually just a drop in each spot. Oil at the beginning of a sewing session, instead of the end, so the oil can work its way into the mechanisms.

• Change the needles

Serger needles will wear out more quickly than those on your conventional machine, due to the speed of the machine. Needles with sharp, smooth points are essential to good stitch quality. Change them every third garment or project, or more often if they are noticeably bent or burred. Sometimes just changing to a different size needle improves stitch quality. Just be sure you have the right **type** needle for your model (see page 20).

• Change the knife blades

When the trimmed edge is ragged, check that the knives are aligned and secured properly. If so, probably one or both blades are dull. One is made of an alloy steel that is very hard and rarely needs changing. The other is softer and more likely to be damaged if you accidentally serge into a pin. On some machines the softer blade is the moveable upper knife and on some it is the stationary lower blade. Thick fabrics and synthetics dull blades faster.

Decorative Serging

CHAPTER 8

DECORATIVE SERGING

Sergers open a whole new world of decorative sewing. Gail has always sewn creatively, but **even** Pati, who generally prefers classic traditional sewing, has discovered the fun of creative decorative serging.

Whenever serging shows, it is decorative, even in regular thread. Serging will show more, though, if you shorten the stitch, use a contrasting color thread or a shiny thread of silk or rayon. To make serging even **more** decorative, use pearl cotton, metallic and other novelty threads, yarns and ribbons described in this chapter.

Be adventurous! Experiment! Even minor tension adjustments can make a major change in the finished look of the stitch. Sew test samples...so buy lots of thread! Testing is not only essential to successful decorative serging, but it is also the way to discover NEW decorative effects.

Mix colors and thread types for interesting variations. For example, red crochet thread could be used in the upper looper, black topstitching thread in the lower looper and black all-purpose thread in the needle. Consider whether both sides of the stitch will show when deciding on thread choices.

In this chapter, we will show you where you can use decorative serging, how sewing order must change when the thread shows, and how to use the heavier threads in your machine.

DECORATIVE SERGING WITH HEAVIER THREADS, YARNS AND RIBBONS

You'll be amazed at the beautiful stitches that can be formed by serging with heavier threads, cords and ribbons. Understanding the types most suitable for decorative serging and how they can be used is essential to trouble-free stitching. Remember that these novelty threads are usually used in combination with all-purpose or serger thread to form the stitch.

Generally, the decorative threads can be categorized into silkies, metallics, bulkies and ribbons, each with their own set of characteristics.

SILKIES include all threads that are soft and shiny. They may be of silk; but more likely, their fiber content is rayon. Silk is very strong, but is also relatively expensive. More stores are beginning to carry it again. Rayon has silk's luster, and is more affordable and more available. Both come in fine and thicker weights. Both take dyes very well, so are available in an array of vibrant colors as well as neutrals. Rayon machine embroidery thread also comes in several variegated shades.

Decor 6, available to home-sewers and retailers through Palmer/ Pletsch, is a soft, heavyweight rayon thread that is washable and colorfast. Because it's an untwisted yarn, it has exceptional luster for a more elegant look; but it is also a little fragile. For this reason, we don't recommend it (or other untwisted threads) for garments that will get extremely heavy wear unless used in a rolled edge, but it is fine for better clothing that will receive TLC.

METALLICS include all threads which contain metallic or metalized fibers, most often blended with another fiber. Like the silky group, they range from fine to heavy weights. The bulkier quality of metallic yarn, a blend of rayon and polyester, makes it a little trickier to use; but it imparts a bolder, more defined edge to medium- and heavyweight fabrics. Brand names include Candlelight by YLI and Glamour by Madeira.

Gold and silver are universally available, but metallics can also be found in a range of jewel tones plus iridescent and variegated shades. Remember the metallic fiber could irritate the skin—plan your decorative serging accordingly. Most metallic threads can be washed and dry-cleaned.

BULKIES is a large category that includes threads with a matte finish that are thicker than regular serger thread, from the relatively lightweight topstitching thread all the way to yarn.

Topstitching thread is a highly-twisted cord-like thread, also known as buttonhole twist. Because it is only a little heavier than regular serger thread, it is among the easiest to use for decorative serging. It is widely available in many colors.

Woolly Nylon was introduced to the home-sewing market by YLI in 1984. Since then, other companies have begun offering similar texturized nylon threads, such as Bulky Lock from Coats & Clark and Metroflock from Wrights/Swiss-Metrosene. All are 100% nylon with a crimped, fuzzy quality that makes them resemble wool.

Texturized nylon can be compared to a curled lock of hair. Just as a lock is made up of many hairs curled together, a strand of texturized nylon is made up of many filaments heat-crimped together. When the lock (strand) is stretched, the hair (thread) is straight and thin; but when it relaxes, it fluffs and spreads. Thus, texturized nylon provides a bulky look without the bulk.

Texturized nylon "fills in" to cover an edge. Its untwisted quality, however, makes it prone to snagging. Because of its nylon fiber content, use a low iron temperature and a press cloth when pressing over the stitching.

This thread can also serve a practical function when used in the needle as well. Its inherent stretchiness actually "tightens up" the seam, making a VERY STRONG seam that won't pull apart. In addition, the thread's soft feel makes it more comfortable next to the skin. It's ideal for sewing activewear.

Crochet thread is a strong, highly-twisted cord, available in either cotton or acrylic. The acrylic variety is similar to cotton but fuzzier, making it an ideal coordinate for wools and sweater knits. Coats & Clark makes Knit-Cro-Sheen in both fiber contents as well as with a metallic twist, and offers it in 175-yard balls. You're most likely to find it in craft and variety stores.

Pearl cotton comes in two sizes for serger use—#8 (finer) and #5 (thicker). Both are loosely twisted, yielding a soft sheen. Available in a broad range of colors plus variegated shades, it can be found in 10-yard skeins or 50-yard balls. In addition, Coats & Clark now offers 150-yard cones of pearl cotton #5 with a special finish applied to the thread to make it easier to use in the serger.

Punch-needle threads and yarns, such as Madeira's Burmilana, are available in two weights. The finer one is as easy to use as topstitching thread, while the heavy weight presents challenges similar to pearl cotton #5. Their acrylic fiber content, however, makes them resemble wool.

Yarn is the most difficult of all to use in the serger, but you can make it work if you choose one that is fine, smooth, tightly twisted and strong. Check the weight by running two strands through the looper eye. If you can't force a double strand through, then you can assume that one strand would not feed easily enough to work successfully. TEST!

RIBBONS produce a braid-like serged edging, as long as they are narrow, soft and pliable, such as 1/8" silk, rayon or silky acrylic knitting ribbons. Most of the ribbons that you find on rolls in fabric stores, by contrast, have thick selvages that make them too stiff for use in the serger. Ribbon Thread and Ribbon Floss are two products that look like ribbon but sew like thread.

NYLON MONOFILAMENT is a clear thread with a "plastic" quality, but newer versions are much softer than their wiry predecessors. They can be used in the needle or loopers whenever you want the thread to be "invisible."

Wrights/Swiss-Metrosene offers a very fine polyester thread called Metrolene. Available in several translucent colors, it is more thread-like, but exhibits a nearly invisible quality like the clear nylon.

TROUBLE-FREE DECORATIVE SERGING TIPS

TEST, TEST, TEST!!! Try stitch width, length, tension and pressure settings on scraps first. Two adjustments are nearly always necessary: 1) a longer stitch length to compensate for the thickness of the decorative thread, and 2) loosening of the tension(s) for smooth feeding (some machines work best if the thread, yarn, or ribbon is taken completely out of the tension dial).

Try these tips for decorative serging:

- Use specialty threads in the upper looper because usually that thread is "on top" and is the one that shows. Fewer threads work successfully in the **lower looper** because its extra thread guides add stress. If the overlock stitch must be reversible choose a thread that will work well in **both** loopers.

- If using the decorative thread in the needle, use a needle with an eye that is large enough to accommodate the thread without causing it to fray.

- Use a new needle. Because of the serger speed, the needle may be "tired" even though you may not feel a burr on the tip.

- Use a needle threader or a dental floss threader (from your local drug store) to easily thread larger threads through the hole.

- Place your fabric under the presser foot and hold thread tails lightly when starting to sew.

- SEW SLOWLY—especially when using thick threads.

- Decorative threads, yarns and ribbons must **feed easily** as you serge to avoid uneven stitching. Many novelty threads are not wound on spools. To facilitate smooth feeding:

  - Rewind onto cones or spools, but wind carefully. Rewinding adds tension to the thread, causing uneven stitches. "Crosswind" by moving the spool back and forth.

    hand wind yarn on empty cone.

  - Place the ball or skein in a bowl next to the machine or on the floor. Then simply reel off a large quantity and serge—reel and serge—reel and serge. Just be sure there is always a loose "pool" of thread available. Try "snaking" the pool behind your machine.

EXPOSED SERGED SEAMS

Exposed seams are common in sportswear and designer sweaters. Sonia Rykiel is known for using exposed seams on wool jersey and cotton knit dresses. You'll see this look in many fabrics, from sweatshirting to lightweight cottons. Exposed seams are also **perfect for baby clothes**, because the seams are **away from** baby's sensitive skin.

We like the look of a 3 or 3/4-thread stitch. Because the seams stick out, you may prefer all-purpose thread in both the loopers and the needles for the same look on each side of the seam.

Serge wrong sides together.

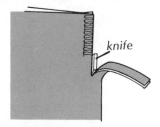

knife

For added durability, you can topstitch the serged seam flat to the garment.

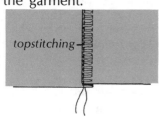

topstitching

DECORATIVE EDGES

Would you like to eliminate trimming, grading, turning, and pressing of collars, cuffs, and faced necklines? Single layer construction or two layers stitched WRONG sides together, like a facing to a neckline, would be unthinkable without a serger. It's easy and suitable for any type of fabric, from sheers to double-faced wools, knits or wovens.

To convert a style to single layer construction, you will need to decide where you will use serged edges and then whether or not you'll need the extra body of the facing behind it.

STABILIZING EDGES

If any edge needs stabilizing try the following: face, interface, serge over ribbon placed on the wrong side, or serge over decorative thread or yarn placed on the right side.

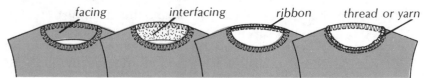

facing   interfacing   ribbon   thread or yarn

SEWING ORDER FOR DECORATIVE SERGING

The fastest way to finish edges is to serge over your first stitches for an inch or two, then chain off the edge.

A simple top like this with 4 circular edges could look very untidy. On page 45, we showed you a neater way to do it, but it is time consuming.

The solution? Avoid sewing in circles. Plan your sewing order so you finish the edges before the last seam. Use the sewing order shown for this easy top with exposed seams and serged edges.

1. Sew shoulder seam.

2. Finish neckline, then edge of sleeve.

3. Sew other shoulder seam. Then finish other sleeve edge.

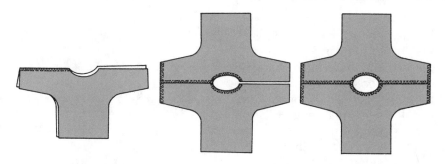

4. Sew side seam.

5. Finish hem.

6. Sew other side seam. Tie off at X's, then secure the ends of the seam. (See page 38.)

USE EXPOSED SEAMS AND EDGES

Casual tops

Use a single layer of interlock, jersey and lightweight double knit or woven fabrics. Finish edges with decorative serging using any thread type. If edges stretch, lighten the presser foot pressure.

Jackets

Use a single layer of melton cloth, double-faced wool and sweaterknits. Edge finish collar and lapel first, then serge collar to the neckline. For lapels, a balanced stitch with the same thread on both loopers, will facilitate continuous serging.

Sheer to lightweight blouses

Use voile, crepe de chine, handkerchief linen, and lightweight cottons and cotton blends. Eliminate facings and use single layer construction. Use a narrow rolled or unrolled hem on all edges including collars. Be sure to edge finish the collars before attaching to the neckline. You can even sew invisible seams in these fabrics using a narrow rolled edge to sew the two layers together.

Reversibles

A wide range of fabrics are suitable from silk to denims. This works well for a child's jumper as well as for a blouse with turned back contrast lapels. Serge the two layers together with a narrow satin stitch.

Fast Shirts

Gail made the Palmer/ Pletsch 3-Hour Shirt in TWO HOURS! She did it by serging off the entire seam allowances of the collar, cuff, front band and pocket, then lapping and stitching. She even serged and lapped the "painless placket" sleeve seam.

A few tips . . .

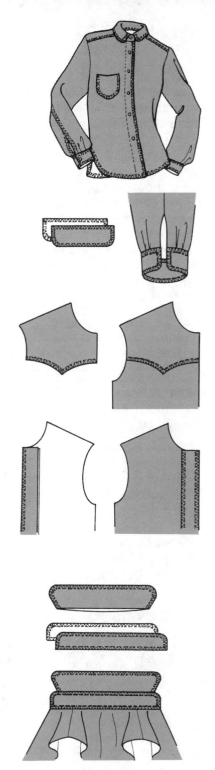

- **Cuffs** — Serge around all edges of both the cuff and cuff facing. Sandwich the sleeve between the cuffs and edgestitch all sides with a conventional machine.

- **Yokes** — Serge the lower edges of the yokes and topstitch to garment with a conventional machine.

- **Front bands** — Cut band into two strips. Serge bands WRONG sides together to wrong side of front. Then serge other edges of band together.

- **Patch pockets** — Cut with top edge on fold. Serge edges and topstitch to shirt. On heavier fabrics, cut pockets single layer and serge all edges.

- **Collar and collar bands** — Wrong sides together, serge outer edges of upper and under collar together. Round off collar points for easier, continuous stitching.

- **Attaching collar/collar bands/ and neckline** — Sandwich collar and neckline edges between bands and edgestitch on conventional machine.

THE 2-HOUR TOP WITH DECORATIVE LAPPED SEAMS

Thanks to sergers, lapped seams, such as those used in sewing Ultrasuede brand fabrics, are possible on woven fabrics. Use the decorative thread, yarn or ribbon of your choice in the upper looper. First serge edges, then lap and topstitch.

Lynn Raasch, a Palmer/Pletsch seminar instructor, made this simple top in two hours. Copy her idea with any similar pattern. She chose multi-colored raw silk suiting cut on the bias. She edgestitched with a pearl cotton that matched one of the colors in the fabric. The result was smashing...truly a designer look!

1. Serge edges as shown, trimming away seam allowances.

2. If edges need stabilizing, try one of the methods suggested on page 60.

3. Finish underlap edges by serging with regular thread or with a line of seam sealant.

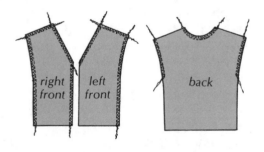

right front   left front   back

4. Lap the serged edge over the corresponding garment piece to the seam line. Tuck thread chains between layers. Edge or topstitch (make a TEST sample): 1) center front; 2) shoulders; 3) one side seam; 4) hem; and 5) other side seam).

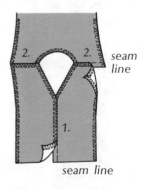

seam line

FINISH EDGES WITH RIBBON

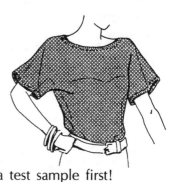

ribbon

hem or
seam
line

Rather than hemming a skirt, sleeve bottom or the edge of a ruffle, place $1/16''$ to $1/4''$ satin or grosgrain ribbon on the right side of the garment next to the hem or seam line. Set your stitch width slightly wider than the ribbon and long enough for the ribbon to show through. Serge from the right side over the ribbon, cutting off the seam or hem allowance. Be careful not to cut the ribbon.

The same idea can apply to stabilizing an edge, like in this open weave mesh top. Place the ribbon on the wrong side of your fabric along the hem or seam line, and serge right side up over the ribbon. This works best on straight edges, but will work on **slightly** curved edges. Make a test sample first!

TRIMS, BELTS, AND HAIR RIBBONS

If you can't find coordinating trims or belts, serge over ribbon, middy or soutache braid, or yarn using thread in the color(s) of your fabric. Braid several together for a belt or Chanel-like trim. Children LOVE custom designed hair ribbons.

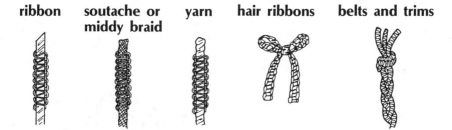

| ribbon | soutache or middy braid | yarn | hair ribbons | belts and trims |

DECORATIVE TOPSTITCHING

If you have a 4-thread serger, use the straight chainstitch for decorative topstitching. Use it for edgestitching jeans and table linens and even to sew tucks. Thread pearl cotton in the lower looper and stitch with the wrong side of the fabric up, so the decorative thread will be on the right side.

FLATLOCKED SEAMS

Flatlocking is joining two layers of fabric with a serged seam, then pulling the two layers apart until the seam lies flat.

2-thread flatlocking — This is the easiest to do!
It **may** be necessary to slightly loosen the needle and looper tensions for the flattest look. Test first!

To have loops on the outside: Sew two layers of fabric **wrong** sides together; then pull on the two layers until the seam is flat.

To have the ladder on the outside: Sew two layers of fabric **right** sides together; then pull on the two layers until the seam is flat.

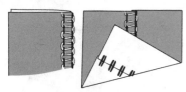

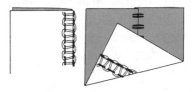

3-thread flatlocking — Loosen the needle tension nearly all the way. Tighten the lower looper tension until the loops disappear and form a straight line along the edge of the fabric. The upper looper tension may need to be loosened slightly to help the fabric flatten, especially if the fabric is thick or the upper looper thread is heavy. Practice with three colors of threads until you master 3-thread flatlocking.

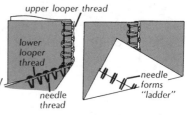

upper looper thread

lower looper thread

needle thread

needle forms "ladder"

If your fabric ravels, fold seam allowances under first. Allow stitches to hang off the edges of the folds. That way you don't have to worry about cutting the folds and the fabric will be easier to flatten.

FLATLOCKED TOPSTITCHING

Fold your fabric and flatlock the edge being careful not to cut the fold. Pull the fabric flat. VOILA! . . . decorative "topstitching."

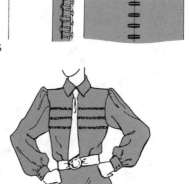

Fold wrong sides together for loops to show on the right side. Fold right sides together for ladder to show on the right side.

Also use flatlocking when fringing loosely woven fabrics. Fold at the point to which you will fringe. Flatlock "topstitch" the fold as described above. Fringe to the flatlocking.

FLATLOCKED HEMS

Flatlocking works best for straight or moderately curved hems. Remove knife or be careful not to cut hem fold while serging. Adjust tensions as described in flatlocked seams page 66.

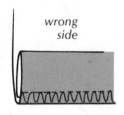

To have the loops on the right side:

1. Turn up hem allowance to WRONG side.

2. Press. Turn up hem again so cut edge is firmly inside and fold. Pin to hold.

3. With the hem allowance down, flatlock next to the fold, being careful not to cut it while stitching.

4. Pull the hem down until stitching is flat.

To have the ladder on the right side:

1. Turn up the hem allowance to the WRONG side.

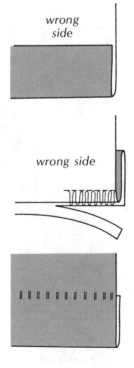

2. Then fold hem width less ¼″ to RIGHT side. Flatlock close to the fold, being careful not to cut it, yet trimming off some of the hem edge to finish it.

3. Pull the hem down until the stitching is flat.

Fast Fashion Details

CHAPTER 9

FAST FASHION DETAILS

If you love to sew, but seldom find the time, read this chapter! Find out how even difficult details can be fun, fast, and easy with a serger. In this chapter you will find tips on:

bands	hems	shoulder pads
belt loops	lettuce leaf edging	special seams
buttons	plackets	spaghetti straps
collars	pockets	tucks and pin tucks
gathers	ribbing	waistbands
	ruffles and trims	

SELF-FABRIC BANDS

Bands can add dramatic color accents and are lightweight edge finishes for knits and wovens. With a serger, they can be applied and finished in one step.

Use your pattern to cut the bands to size. Lightweight fusible non-woven or knit interfacing is optional. Seam as necessary. Fold the bands in half, wrong sides together.

Pin to the garment, distributing ease evenly, then serge. The seam is beautifully finished, automatically extends toward the garments, and only light pressing is necessary.

BELT LOOPS

Serge the edges of belt loops for a decorative or sporty look.

For lighter weight fabrics, cut the loops **double layer as shown**. Serge the edges trimming about ¼" off each side. Experiment on scraps to determine the loop width and stitch width desired. The narrower your finished loops, the narrower you'll want the edge stitching. Cut the loops and sew to garment.

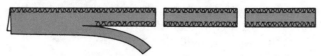

NOTE: On heavier fabrics like coatings, cut the loops single layer.

THREAD BELT LOOPS

1. Set machine on narrow or rolled edge, and a short stitch length. You may also use polyester top-stitching thread in the needle and looper(s) for a more durable loop.

2. Hold the thread tail lightly and sew a continuous chain long enough for all of your loops plus seam allowances.

3. Thread the chain through a needle with a large eye or a self-threading needle, as shown.

4. Pull chain from inside to outside to inside of garment.

5. To secure, knot chain just inside the garment, plus knot ends of chain together.

inside | outside
of garment | of garment

knot

inside of garment | outside of garment

knot

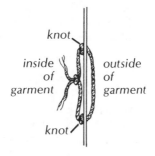

BUTTONS

The following buttons coordinate with your fabric and decorative edges. They look great on coats and sweaters.

1. For each button, cut a triangle 1" × 7" or to a size suitable for your fabric. Serge along the long edges. Chain off at the point and secure thread with seam sealant.

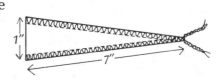

1"

7"

2. Roll up the triangle beginning at the wide end.

3. Sew button to garment at the point of the triangle.

COLLARS

Quick convertible collars

Eliminate back neck facings and hand sewing the neck edge of blouses with convertible collars.

1. Straighten the neck edge by staystitching next to seam line and clipping to stitches.

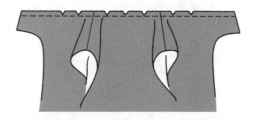

2. Place collar on neckline. Serge the ends of the facings.

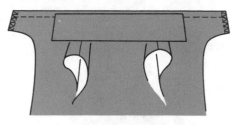

3. Fold in facings along fold line. Serge the neck seam. Turn right sides out.

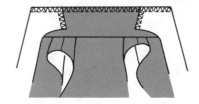

NOTE: If corners are too bulky, reinforce with 2″ of stitching on conventional machine, then trim and grade.

Quick Peter Pan collars

We first saw this method of collar application used in children's clothing and decided it could be used in adult clothing too! There are no facings and the serged seam lies under the collar leaving a clean edge around the neckline.

Because the garment will have either a facing or centered zipper, finish the top edge up to the collar before applying the collar.

1. Staystitch on both sides of the collar dot. Clip to dot.

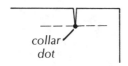

collar
dot

2. Fold right sides together, along foldline. Stitch.

3. Trim seam and slash corner. Turn to right side.

4. Pin right side of finished collar to wrong side of garment.

5. Serge collar to garment at neckline seam.

6. Flip collar to right side.

GATHERS

Use your serger to gather. Pull on the needle thread (the shortest one in the chain) of a 3-thread stitch. OR, tighten the needle tension and it will automatically gather. To gather more, use a longer stitch length, differential feed set at 2, and lighter weight fabrics.

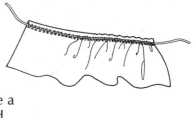

You can also gather by serging over cording. This works well for yards and yards of ruffles. Some machines have a special cording foot that feeds the cord into the middle of the stitch automatically.

HEMS

We will show you **9 DIFFERENT WAYS** to hem on your serger. Choose one of the following for the bottom of your skirts, pants, sleeves or blouses.

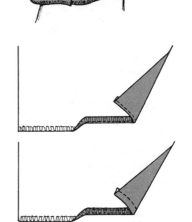

- **The no-hem hem**
  Leave tuck-in blouses unhemmed for the smoothest hipline. Serge the edge with a medium width and length stitch. Press to make very flat.

- **Easy hem for full skirts**
  Right side up, serge the lower edge with a medium width and length stitch. Turn serging to wrong side and edgestitch.

- **Shirt hem**
  Right side up, serge the edge with a medium width and length stitch. Turn serging to wrong side and topstitch ¼" from edge.

NOTE: Tightening the lower looper (or needle on a 2-thread) slightly will help curl the edge under making the edge easier to press up.

4. Eased hem

For wider turned up hems on A-line skirts, ease the edge and finish it in one step. Loosen the needle thread tension and pull up on it. Topstitch or handstitch the hem.

5. Blind hem

Fold hem up and back. While finishing the edge, barely catch the fold. Use a longer stitch length. If stitches show on right side, call it a "sport" hem.

6. Flatlocked hem

Fold hem up and back with fold and raw edge even. Flatlock as on page 67, being careful not to cut fold.

7. Mock band hem

Fold hem up and back. Sew a 3 or 3/4-thread serged seam, barely cutting off the fold.

8. Narrow rolled and un-rolled hem

These are best for full skirts in lightweight fabrics. The rolled is slightly heavier and more durable, than unrolled hems. Make a test sample. See pages 43-44 for how-to's.

9. Lettuce leaf hem

Crossgrain soft knits and bias wovens will stretch when sewing a narrow rolled or unrolled satin hem with a 2 or 3-thread stitch. Increasing pressure increases the stretch and lettuce leaf effect. Some knits may require stretching to be "leafier."

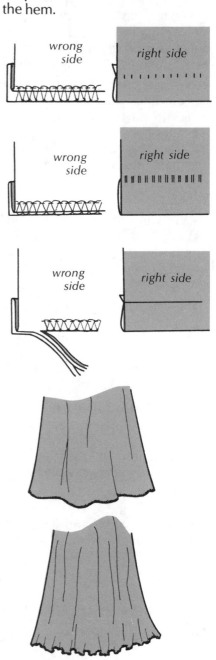

LETTUCE LEAF EDGING

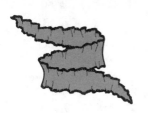

You'll love this wavy look on two-way stretch fabrics, edges of single-layer ribbings, interlocks, lightweight jerseys and tricot. It also works on bias wovens. Use it on ruffles, collars, sleeves, top and skirt hems, and belts.

You can create a lettuce leaf effect with any narrow rolled or unrolled satin stitch on the stretchiest edge of a fabric. The degree of ruffling will vary with the fabric (stretchier types will lettuce more), the grain (crosswise or bias will stretch most), thread density (the more thread, the more ruffling), and the foot pressure (the more foot pressure, the more stretching of the edge). To increase the lettuce leaf effect, the fabric edge can also be gently stretched (be careful not to bend the needle).

QUICK CONTINUOUS PLACKETS

1. Slash your fabric at the placket opening.

2. Serge edge, trimming nothing. When knife reaches corner, with needle down, lift presser foot.

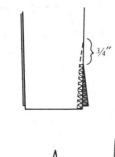

3. Straighten out fabric forming a pleat and serge over edge. Don't worry . . . pleat is temporary.

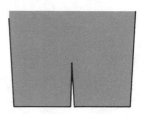

4. Right sides together, straight stitch a ¾" dart at the top of the placket.

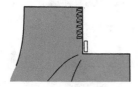

¾"

5. Press full width of serged edge to wrong side. Attach cuff.

SERGED "PAINLESS PLACKET"

If you have a cuffed sleeve with a "painless placket," you can get professional cuff results FAST on a serger. Find a pattern that has a sleeve seam that becomes the placket. Or, convert any sleeve to a "painless placket" sleeve using the instructions in **Mother Pletsch's Painless Sewing**. (See page 128)

1. Serge the sleeve seam allowances if the fabric ravels. Make your cuff.

2. Place cuff to right side of sleeve. Fold placket ends over end of cuff. Serge the seam.

3. Stitch sleeve seam to placket opening. Topstitch placket ¼" from placket opening edges to finish.

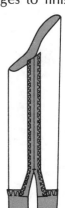

SIDE SEAM POCKETS

There are some fashion details that require the use of both your serger and conventional machine, such as side seam pockets. Follow these easy steps.:

1. Serge pockets to garment. Straight stitch from top to dot. Backstitch. Change to a longer stitch and machine baste to lower dot. Backstitch and continue on 3-4". Glue stick the edges of the pockets together, especially important if they are out of a slippery lining.

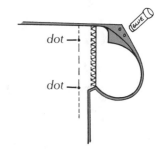

2. Now serge side seam from the lower edge up to the straight stitching. then angle off toward pocket. Serge around pocket. Serge pocket and seam toward front. Remove basting to open pocket.

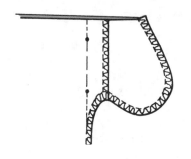

PATCH POCKETS

Pockets can be serged to a garment with a 2-thread flatlock stitch. Make a TEST SAMPLE to make sure you like the results. You may find it easier to serge the edges and topstitch the pocket in place.

1. Press under seam allowances on pocket edges. Place pocket on garment. (Use water soluble glue stick to hold it.)

2. Fold garment back until slightly under pocket edge. Flatlock (see page 66), beginning at very top edge of pocket being careful not to cut the fold. At bottom, clear the stitch fingers (page 47), angle fabric, and chain off the edge. Leave a 3-4" chain at all corners.

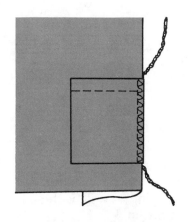

3. Repeat for all three sides of the pocket. Pull pocket flat. Unravel chains. Pull threads to wrong side using a large needle. Tie knots at each corner and dot them with seam sealant. Cut off thread tails.

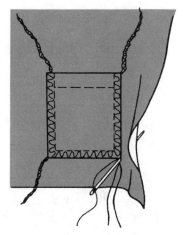

RIBBING

A serged seam stretches with the ribbing, eliminating the prevalent problem of popped seams. Use your pattern to cut correct length of ribbing. Seam as necessary. Pin to the garment, distributing ease evenly.

Then, with the ribbing on top, serge it to the garment, stretching it in front of the foot.

For a fast sewing order when using ribbing, see page 106.

RUFFLES AND TRIMS

Save money by making yards and yards of self-fabric ruffles and trims. Let the serger do the cutting as well as the edge-finishing!

Use the seam width guide on your machine or draw lines on your fabric with a washable marker for even trim widths. Let your serger cut and finish one edge in one step. Then serge the other edge if desired for flat trims.

NOTE: Gather ruffles with a ruffler on your conventional machine. It makes gathering yard after yard of serged ruffles fast and automatically even. Or, use serger gathering method on page 73.

Center-gathered ruffles

Narrow center-gathered ruffles are a nice accent above a flounce on a full skirt or curtains. The ruffle edges can be beautifully hemmed before gathering using a narrow rolled serged hem.

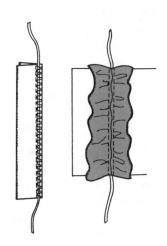

1. Fold fabric in half, right sides together. Serge over cording, being careful not to cut the fold.

2. Pull up the cord and open ruffle. Stitch to fabric on both sides of cord, or zigzag down the middle.

SHOULDER PADS

Buy ready-made pads or make your own using a pattern. Cover them with self-fabric or lining the color of your garment, or, in skin tones for sheer fabrics.

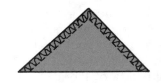

Place the pad on the lining as shown.

Fold the lining over the pad and serge the edges.

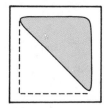

SPECIAL SEAMS

Fast French Seams

A French seam is usually a three step process . . . sew, trim, and sew. With a serger, you can eliminate the trimming step. WRONG sides together serge a ¼" seam ⅜" from the edge. Turn the fabric RIGHT sides together encasing the first seam. Press. Straight stitch ¼" from the edge on your conventional machine.

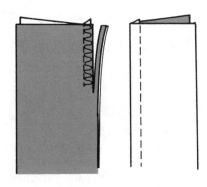

Mock French Seams

Use your rolled edge for sewing a seam in sheer fabrics. They will hardly show, but if they do, the seams will be beautifully finished and an even narrow width.

Mock Flat Felled Seams

This seam is great for heavy coatings. Trim one seam allowance to ¼" and serge the other barely trimming the edge. Then topstitch the seams flat from the right side.

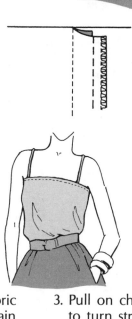

EASY SPAGHETTI STRAPS OR NARROW TIES

Pati made this simple camisole and used the serger to make her narrow spaghetti straps. Use a regular 3-thread stitch. If straps are **very** narrow, use a narrow rolled edge stitch.

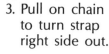

1. Without fabric in machine, serge a chain 6" longer than your strap. Lay chain centered on right side of fabric.

2. Fold fabric over chain and serge strap seam.

3. Pull on chain to turn strap right side out.

TUCKS AND PIN TUCKS

Your serging will show on these decorative tucks. If using a heavier decorative thread, determine which direction your tucks will be pressed before sewing (it will make a difference whether your decorative thread is in the upper or lower looper). Try gold metallic thread on white handkerchief linen — gorgeous!

The easiest way is to tuck the fabric before cutting out the garment, using the following instructions:

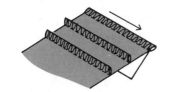

1. Press mark the tuck fold lines. Tucks are generally pressed all in the same direction or toward the sides.

2. Serge along the foldline being careful not to cut the folded edge (raise or remove your knife if you can). Use a narrow stitch for pin tucks and a wider one for regular tucks.

WAISTBANDS

Use this technique in fly front pants to minimize bulk across the tummy. Instead of stitching and turning the end of the underlap side of waistband, just serge the end off. It's flatter and more flattering.

PULL ON WAISTBANDS

Get the ease and comfort of pull-ons with the look of a tailored waistband.

1. Cut band. Seam and press in half according to your pattern instructions.

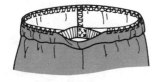

2. Serge the band to the garment, leaving 1-2" unstitched for inserting the elastic.

3. Insert elastic, lap ends and stitch.

4. Serge remainder of band to garment.

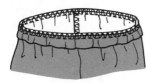

finish
sewing

CHAPTER 10

MAXIMIZING SERGER USE — PATTERN IDEAS

You've learned about serged seams, hems, finishes, decorative edges and fashion details . . . here are some ways the serger techniques can be applied to the latest pattern designs.

Remember, there are special serger patterns (with directions for overlock sewing), but any pattern can be sewn faster and more professionally with a serger. When looking at pattern designs, ask these questions: Can facings be replaced with serged edges? Can a jacket lining be eliminated if seams and hem edges are serged? Could 3, 3/4 or 4-thread serging replace conventional seaming? Can seams be serged and worn "out" as is so popular in readymade knitwear? Could serging be used as a decorative finish? Can single layer construction be used throughout, finishing with rolled edges and decorative serging? The following illustrations will give you some ideas. Be creative. The more you maximize serger use, the more you'll minimize sewing time!

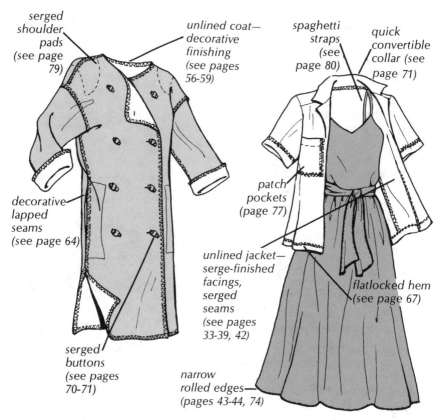

serged shoulder pads (see page 79)

unlined coat— decorative finishing (see pages 56-59)

spaghetti straps (see page 80)

quick convertible collar (see page 71)

decorative lapped seams (see page 64)

patch pockets (page 77)

serged buttons (see pages 70-71)

unlined jacket— serge-finished facings, serged seams (see pages 33-39, 42)

flatlocked hem (see page 67)

narrow rolled edges— (pages 43-44, 74)

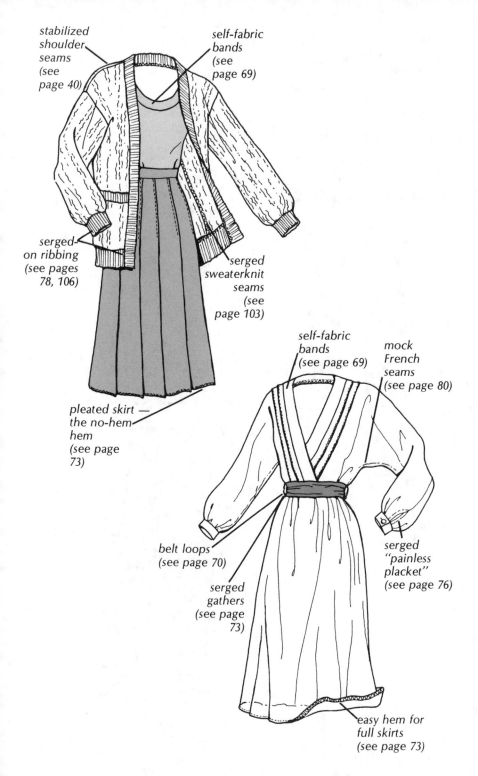

stabilized shoulder seams (see page 40)

self-fabric bands (see page 69)

serged-on ribbing (see pages 78, 106)

serged sweaterknit seams (see page 103)

pleated skirt — the no-hem hem (see page 73)

self-fabric bands (see page 69)

mock French seams (see page 80)

belt loops (see page 70)

serged gathers (see page 73)

serged "painless placket" (see page 76)

easy hem for full skirts (see page 73)

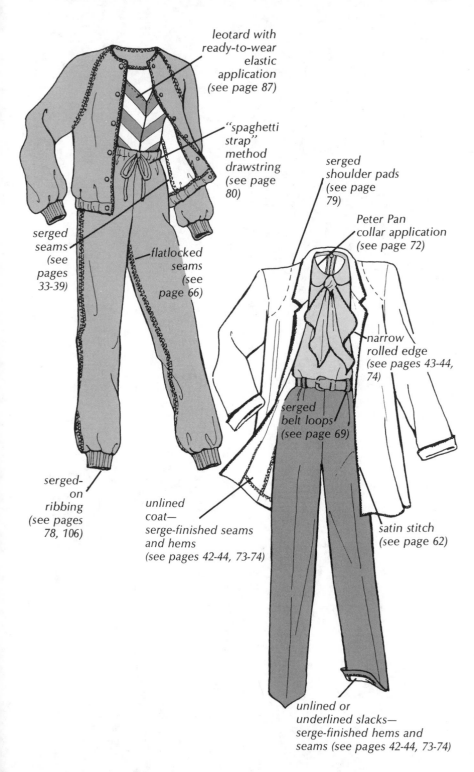

leotard with ready-to-wear elastic application (see page 87)

"spaghetti strap" method drawstring (see page 80)

serged shoulder pads (see page 79)

Peter Pan collar application (see page 72)

serged seams (see pages 33-39)

flatlocked seams (see page 66)

narrow rolled edge (see pages 43-44, 74)

serged belt loops (see page 69)

serged-on ribbing (see pages 78, 106)

unlined coat— serge-finished seams and hems (see pages 42-44, 73-74)

satin stitch (see page 62)

unlined or underlined slacks— serge-finished hems and seams (see pages 42-44, 73-74)

Serging Aerobic
AND SWIMWEAR

CHAPTER 11
SERGING AEROBIC AND SWIMWEAR

Take a close look at ready-made leotards, tights and swimwear. You'll see that serging is synonomous with sewing two-way stretch fabrics. Overlocked seams stretch with the fabrics, eliminate popped out seams, and add "give-with-you" comfort. Best yet, most projects can be finished in a mere **hour or two**! The pretty, practical results speak for themselves!

Had trouble finding leotard and swimsuit patterns? Look again in major pattern company catalogues. Many have added more swimsuits (for kids too) and the newest leotard/tight ensembles. Some smaller pattern companies specialize in two-way stretch styles, including Kwik Sew, Patch Press, Prime Moves and Stretch and Sew.

THREAD

Ready-to-wear manufacturers often use "woolly nylon" thread (see page 26) when serging swim and aerobicwear. The woolly nylon is strong but stretchier than other thread types and produces a softer seam, desirable in body fitting fashions. Ask about it at your serger dealer, or inquire with mail order thread specialists.

NEEDLES

If using nylon/spandex (Lycra®) you may find ball point needles less damaging to the fabric. Sew a TEST SAMPLE.

SEAMS

Aerobicwear and swimwear seams must stretch. A 3-thread overlock produces the stretchiest seam (with a 3/4-thread stitch a close second) but **any serger will sew this category beautifully**.

Actually, even a serged chainstitch (like in a true 4-thread stitch), stretches more than a conventional straight stitch. To build more stretch into the 4-thread chainstitch, sew with woolly nylon thread (see page 26).

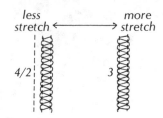

No matter what serger you are using, a well-balanced stitch (see page 50) will be the strongest and stretchiest, important in tight-fitting two-way stretch fashions. Check the needle tension. If it is too tight, the seam will be less stretchy.

EASY READY-TO-WEAR ELASTIC APPLICATION

Serged-on elastic is a professional technique most ready-to-wear manufacturers use. The elastic will never bunch or twist during wearing or washing, and the fullness is controlled where you need it.

1. Cut the elastic to the length suggested by the pattern or fit to your body area by "trying on" the elastic. Standard ratios for length of elastic to fabric are 1:1 at necklines and armholes, 1:1 at the front leg and 3:4 at the back leg (or about 2" less elastic than fabric).

2. Serge the elastic to the wrong side of the fabric edge. With the elastic on top, hold all layers behind the foot with your left hand, as you sew. Use your other hand to stretch the elastic to fit the opening.

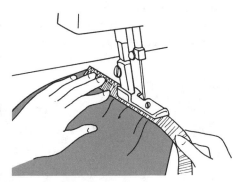

Either a 2-thread overedge or 3-thread overlock can be used to attach the elastic. Stitch length should be long (stitches will be closer when the elastic contracts). Set stitch width medium to wide.

3. Turn the serged edge to the wrong side of the fabric, encasing the elastic.

4. With your conventional machine set on a long stitch (8-10 stitches per inch), topstitch ¼" to ⅜" from the edge stretching as you sew.

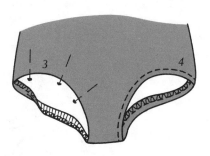

NOTE: For a straight stitch with more give, use a double (twin) needle on your conventional machine. The one bobbin thread which connects the two needle threads forms a "zigzag" on the wrong side.

SEWING ORDER FOR BASIC LEOTARDS AND SWIMSUITS

NOTE: Follow your pattern's fabric stretch guide. For leotards and swimsuits, the stretchiest direction (usually lengthwise grain) goes around the body.

This sewing order will maximize the use of your serger and cut sewing time. Elastic is applied flat, rather than in a circle.

1. Pin fit before serging (safety pin crotch for "ouch-less" fitting).

2. Optional crotch lining for swimsuits:

   a. Serge back, front, and lining seam in one step. Overedge other end of lining.

   b. Serge lining edges to leg edges.

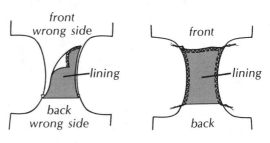

3. Overlock one shoulder seam.

4. Apply elastic to neckline, leg, and armhole openings where required. Serge elastic to within ½" of the open side and shoulder seams.

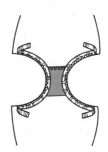

5. Serge the side seams (not catching elastic) and remaining shoulder seam. To avoid bulk and lumpy seams, do not catch elastic in the overlocked seam.

wrong side

6. Lap elastic at the side and shoulder seams and fold under to the wrong side. Pin at seams to secure.

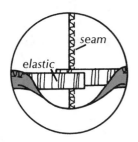

seam

elastic

7. At your conventional machine, place the right side of the garment up. Topstitch (stretching as you sew) the elastic in place around all openings. If desired, use double needle to topstitch (see page 87).

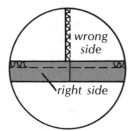

wrong side

right side

LETTUCE LEAF EDGING

You'll love the lettuce leaf finish for edges of belts, neck-lines, sleeves and armholes. See page 75.

EASY ELASTIC BELTS AND STRAPS

These can be made for your aerobic and swimwear instantly on a serger. All stitching is hidden, and the elastic won't twist inside straps. If making a belt, turn ends over buckle fasteners.

1. The width of your finished belt or strap will be the width of your elastic. Cut elastic 3" longer than the belt or strap. Cut your fabric twice the width of the elastic plus ½" and the length needed.

2. Fold fabric in half lengthwise, right sides together. Place elastic on top, even with raw edges. A 3" tail will extend from one end for easy turning.

safety pin   *elastic*

3. After serging through all layers, thread the elastic tail back through the piece using a safety pin. Turn right side out.

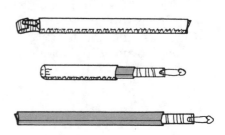

4. The seam will automatically roll to the under side.

TIGHTS

You'll look and feel fantastic in custom-made tights sewn on a serger. In comparison to ready-made tights, they are considerably more durable (no runs!) more supportive (make your legs feel skinny!) and of course, fit better.

You actually use the same two-way stretch fabric recommended for leotards and swimsuits. This heavier tight fabric stands up to a beating . . . those who aerobicize, skate, or ski (used as long underwear) love them! Gail even sees joggers in Eugene, Oregon (Track City USA) wearing nylon/spandex tights in place of warmup pants. Try serging a pair to coordinate with your leotard — it's less than a one-hour task.

SEWING ORDER FOR BASIC TIGHTS

Following your pattern stretch guide is crucial for the proper fitting of tights. The stretchiest grain (usually lengthwise) goes up and down the leg.

You'll discover this sewing order varies from that which is recommended in most patterns. The reason? Sewing the waistband and stirrup seams last allows you to fit as you sew. Too-long stirrup openings, frequently seen on homesewn tights, will be eliminated.

> **NOTE:** Measure and follow your pattern fitting guidelines. If in doubt, cut tights too long. Add 1-2" "fitting insurance" to waistline and stirrup bottom edges. Excess can be trimmed off later.

1. Finish stirrup edges with serging. Elastic is not used here because it would be too bulky.

inseam edge   inseam edge

2. Right sides together, over-lock inner leg seam.

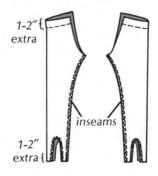

1-2" { extra

inseams

1-2" extra {

3. Overlock the crotch seam, right sides together.

4. Cut elastic to desired length, lap and stitch with a conventional machine.

5. Try on tights, wrong sides out. Pull the tights up under the elastic. Mark next to the top edge of the elastic with washable marker.

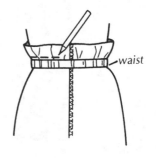

waist

6. Place the elastic on the wrong side of the fabric with lower edge next to markings as shown. Distribute fullness evenly. Serge, stretching elastic to fit the tights.

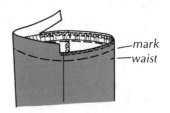

mark
waist

7. Turn the serged edge to the wrong side, encasing the elastic. From the right side, stitch the elastic in place with a zigzag stitch catching all layers. Slightly stretch the elastic as you sew.

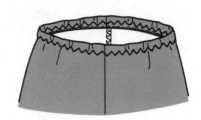

8. Use safety pins to position the correct stirrup length. The fit should be snug without pulling down the crotch or waistline (do some toe touches or run in place to simulate "real" use.

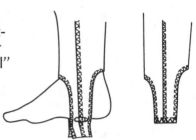

9. Overlock the stirrup seams.

LEG WARMERS

Leg warmers are all the rage! Even if you aren't a professional dancer, this popular aerobic accessory makes you look like one.

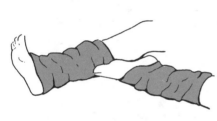

For fabric, use recycled sweaters and sweats, sweaterknit or cotton rib knit. Ribbing works best because it stretches and recovers well. The fabric stretch should go around the leg.

1. Fold each end of the leg warmers to the wrong side about 4-5".

2. Check length and then blind-stitch the hem edge with a 2 or 3-thread serge. (See page 74.)

3. Pin-fit the leg warmer to your leg. Generally the "cuffs" should be tight enough to stay up, but the rest can be to the contour of the leg.

4. Serge the seam.

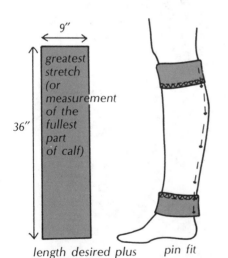

9"

36"

greatest stretch (or measurement of the fullest part of calf)

length desired plus hem allowance (unless ribbed)

pin fit

Lingerie and Lace

CHAPTER 12

LINGERIE AND LACE

In the past we've both wondered why anyone would spend their precious sewing time making underwear. Upon discovering sergers, the answer became obvious — most lingerie can be serged beautifully and professionally in one short sewing session.

If your local fabric store doesn't carry lingerie fabric, check the mail order section of sewing publications or, treat yourself (or that lucky person on your gift list) to elegant custom-fit silk or silky lingerie only seen in expensive designer ready-mades.

BEFORE YOU BEGIN

- Most nylon lingerie tricots will roll LESS if NOT prewashed. Shrinkage is negligible. Real silks can be "wash and wear" if preshrunk. (Refer to **Sensational Silk**, see page 128.)

- If substituting lightweight wovens such as silks or silk-likes for tricots, cut pattern pieces on the bias. The extra give in bias will simulate the tricot knit fit.

- To determine the right side of tricots, stretch the crosswise edge and it will roll to the right side. Mark the right sides of the garment pieces with Scotch® Brand Magic™ Transparent Tape.

NOTE: Because tricot does roll to the right side, serge right side down when hemming with a narrow rolled edge.

FLAT CONSTRUCTION IS FASTER

When working with small circular area, flat construction is faster and easier.

NOTE: If you want a lined or double layer crotch, place the two layers wrong sides together and treat as one.

Try this sewing order for panties:

1. Place crotch and crotch lining wrong sides together. Serge to right sides of front and back.

2. Serge elastic to leg openings.

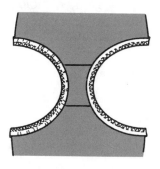

3. Right sides together, serge one side seam.

4. Serge elastic to the waistline.

5. Serge the other side seam, right sides together.

6. Panties are finished.

Half slips can be serged in 30 minutes or less and at a fraction of readymade cost. Try flatlocking both the lace and elastic to your slip fabric. Use tricot or bias wovens. Or, to help a garment hold its shape, use a polyester woven cut on the straight of grain.

Try this easy sewing order for half slips:

1. Serge one side seam.

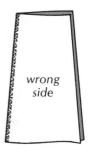

wrong side

2. Serge elastic to the waistline.

right side

3. Serge lace to slip hem.

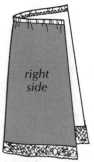

right side

4. Serge the other side seam.

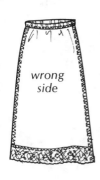

wrong side

ELASTIC APPLICATIONS

Flatlocked elastic

Once the exclusive "secret" of lingerie manufacturers, sewers can now apply elastics directly, in one-step, with minimal bulk and no casings using a flatlocking.

2-thread flatlocking is our favorite for lingerie as it will lie flatter than 3-thread flatlocking. For more on machine settings for flatlocking, see page 66.

To flatlock elastic to lingerie, sew as follows:

1. **For knits,** cut off the seam allowance and place elastic next to the edge of the fabric **right sides together**. Serge from the elastic side being careful not to cut the elastic.

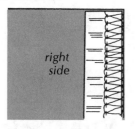

For wovens, first serge the fabric edge to prevent raveling. Then fold the seam allowance to the wrong side for added strength. Place the elastic next to the fold of the fabric **right sides together**. Serge from the elastic side, being careful not to cut the folds or the elastic.

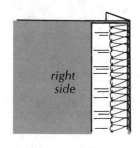

2. Pull the elastic up until the edge of the fabric and the elastic are butted together. There will be a ladder effect on the right side.

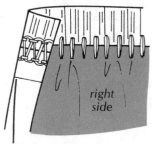

seam
allowance
if using wovens

NOTE: If you want the loops on the right side, stitch with elastic and fabric **wrong sides together**.

Overlocked elastic

This application is more durable than flatlocking, but it is slightly bulkier. This is generally not a problem if soft lingerie elastic is used. Use ½" lingerie elastic and a ¼" serged seam, with either a 3 or 3/4-thread stitch.

1. Leave a ¼" seam allowance on garment.

2. Place the elastic on top of the fabric, **right sides together**. Serge the edges together being careful not to cut the elastic with the knives. Stretch the elastic in front of the needle (see page 87).

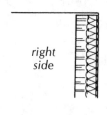

right side

3. Turn elastic up. Push seam allowance toward the garment.

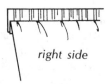

right side

LACE APPLICATIONS

Lace is synonomous with lovely lingerie. We like the following 3 methods of applying lace:

Flatlocked lace

This is a flat, seamless lace application. Follow the same steps described for flatlocked elastic on page 97. Try this tip for holding the lace in place. Tape it to the fabric with Scotch Brand Magic, Transparent Tape®.

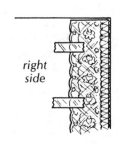

right side

Overlapped lace

1. Trim seam or hem allowances off garment.

2. Serge the edge if fabric is ravely.

3. Lap lace ¼" over the edge of the **RIGHT** side of the garment. Using a straight stitch or narrow zig-zag on your conventional machine, edgestitch the lace in place.

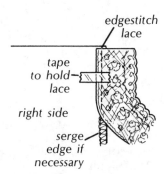

edgestitch lace

tape to hold lace

right side

serge edge if necessary

Attaching lace with ribbon

Serge lace and ribbon to your fabric in one step using the flatlocking method described on page 66 following these steps:

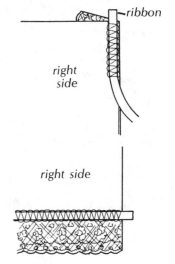

1. Trim seam allowance from garment. Place lace and garment edges wrong sides together.

2. With the garment on top, place ⅛" ribbon along the edge of the RIGHT side of the fabric.

3. Stitch over the ribbon, with a medium stitch width, being careful not to cut the ribbon.

4. Pull on the lace and fabric until they lie flat.

Mock French Hand Sewing

This delicate lace application is great for camisoles, blouses and christening gowns. Create French hand sewn yardage using strips of fabric and lace, then cut out garment.

1. Place lace trim on wrong side of a fabric strip. With lace on top, sew edges together with a narrow rolled hem (page 43).

2. Attach a second fabric strip to other side of lace trim in the same way. Add as many lace inserts as desired.

3. Open up and the inset lace will lie flat.

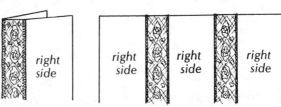

NOTE: Stitching with fabric and lace wrong sides together means the seams (rolled edge pintucks) form on the right side of the fabric. If you'd prefer the seams to be on the under side, serge with right sides together.

MAKE YOUR OWN LACE TRIM

Can't find just the right lace trim or just the right lace fabric to coordinate with trim? Your serger and conventional machine can create the trim and/or yardage you need.

Make lace trim out of lace yardage:

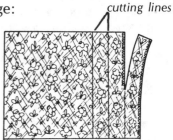
cutting lines

1. Cut out strips as you sew, using narrow rolled or unrolled serging. Use washable marker to draw lines on lace as a guide for cutting even width strips.

2. Finish other edge with same serging stitch.

MAKE YOUR OWN LACE YARDAGE

Make lace yardage out of lace trim (1″ or wider straight edge lace works best):

1. Right sides together, flat-lock or overlock lace, row after row, until the desired size is achieved.

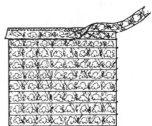

2. Then cut out the garment from the newly created yardage.

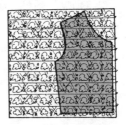

Serging Sweaters

CHAPTER 13

SERGING SWEATERS

Sweater knits can be sewn together and edge finished beautifully with a serger. Gail serges together her **handknits** because the seams are quicker and less bulky than traditional seaming by hand. Pati buys sweater knit yardage and edge finishes with a serger — no more endless searching for matching ribbings!

A serger also opens up exciting new opportunities for assembling and finishing other similar handmade fabrics such as crochets and handwovens. You'll get professional results in record time!

Sweater knit yardage has been scarce in fabric stores. However, because sweaters are such an important fashion look, some retailers are carrying them again. Also, many mail order specialists carry designer or factory mill ends. Consult the "fabric-by-mail" ads in sewing publications.

BEFORE YOU BEGIN

* **Knit or crochet your own sweater yardage.** Then, using a sewing pattern, cut out your sweater with this easy method. (Pati may even take up knitting!) This cut-and-serge sweater method works best for fine to medium (4 or more stitches/inch) cottons, linens, wools, and blends. Silky rayons and real silks can be more ravel prone. To prevent raveling, you can draw around the pattern with chalk or a washable marker before cutting. Then, stitch just inside the cutting line using a narrow, medium length zig-zag to hold the knit loops in place.

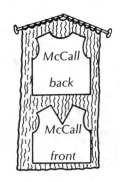

* **"Knit-to-fit" a sewing pattern.** Patterns can streamline the process. Knit or crochet to the shape of a pattern. This eliminates counting stitches and takes the guesswork out of standard knitting or crocheting.

* **Cut sweater knits with ½" to 1" wide seam allowances.** Serging too close to the edges can cause undesirable stretching. The excess will be trimmed off while seaming or finishing.

- **Sew TEST seams on sweater scraps.** The heavier the knit, the wider and longer the stitch should be. Some sergers may have difficulty handling the weight and bulk of heavy sweater knits. Change the knife blade if your serger is cutting ragged edges. Don't use pins—they are too easily buried and forgotten in sweater knits. Running over them damages the knives. Use differential feed set at 2 to prevent stretch if your machine has this feature. Without differential feed, lessen stretching by pushing the fabric into the presser foot with your fingers as you serge.

SWEATER SEAMS

Any serger stitch (except 2-thread overedge alone) works well for seaming sweater knits.

A 3-thread stitch has the most give... great for sweater knit seams that need to stretch.

A 3/4-thread stitch is nearly as stretchy and adds a bit more strength to the seams.

A 4- or 5-thread stitch has little stretch because of the chainstitch. Use it if you want a more stable seam.

  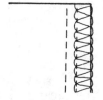

NOTE: Any of these seams can be stabilized using the methods described on pages 40 and 60. They can also become stretchier, if desired, by lightly pulling on the fabric in front of the presser foot.

Try serging with seams on the outside (start with wrong sides together) for a sporty look. It is gorgeous with a coordinating lightweight yarn in the upper looper. See Chapter 8 for more on decorative serging.

FINISHING EDGES

Serging is a perfect finish for sweater knits because it is a "knitting" process and you can use yarns for edges that perfectly coordinate to the sweater knit! See Chapter 8 for more decorative ideas.

STABILIZING EDGES

Many of the raschel sweater knits and loosely constructed handmades require more stabilizing at the edges than just the serged finish. Here are some options:

Facings — Choose compatible jersey, doubleknit or interlock knit to face the edges. Wrong sides together, serge facing to garment. Use lengthwise grain strips for stabilizing straight edges and crosswise or bias for stabilizing curved edges.

NOTE: Fusible knit interfacing can also be fused to the wrong side of edges to stabilize. Try the new stabilized knit fusibles, such as Dritz's Press 'n' Set. Test on a sample first.

For sweater jackets — Cut the facings to the armhole for extra body. (You can then sandwich shoulder pads between facings and the garment.)

Yarn, ribbon, elastic thread, and cording — Serge over any of these, but don't catch them in the stitches. They can then be pulled up, easing for fit or to control edge stretch. Use a darning or yarn needle to draw the tails to the wrong side of the sweater — weave into the sweater knit for 2" or so and clip.

RECYCLING SWEATERS

Remodel and recycle sweaters (especially precious wools and cashmeres) with your serger. This is a FUN way to practice sewing on sweaterknits. You can also make wonderful trims and accessories from old sweaters.

"Sizing down" is the easiest way to remodel. You will have plenty of sweater fabric to work with.

Another way to "size down" is to taper in side seams. Serge deeper seams, tapering into the original seam line.

Too long? Trim off hem ribbing. Then cut off excess length. Serge ribbing back onto sweater, evenly distributing sweater fullness.

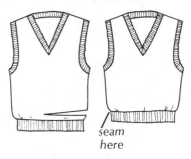

seam here

If there is no ribbing and the sweater is too long, cut off and serge the edge. Then turn up a hem and topstitch.

serge-finish hem

Create patchwork out of old sweaters for a new color blocked or patchwork sweater look. Seams can be on the outside or inside.

CHAPTER 14
CHILDRENSWEAR — SERGER SHORTCUTS

If you have kids, you should own a serger. Serged seams and edge finishes can stand up to the rugged wear and repeated washings subjected to childrenswear. The narrower seam allowances are also in scale with little people sizes. And, as fast as most kids are growing, you need a speedy serger to keep up! Gail tests children's techniques on clothes for her daughter, Bett.

T-SHIRT SEWING ORDER

Kids never have enough cute, comfortable tee shirts. Streamline the cutting and sewing process! Cut and serge one tee in 20 minutes or less with this speedy sewing order:

1. Cut out.

2. Serge one shoulder seam. Then serge ribbing to neckline.

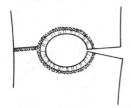

3. Serge the other shoulder seam.
4. Serge the ribbing to sleeve hems.
5. Serge sleeve seams.

6. Serge the one underarm seam.
7. Hem bottom edge with a blind or topstitched hem.
8. Serge the other underarm seam.

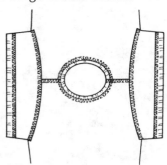

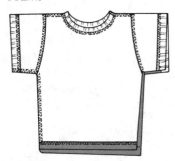

T-SHIRT DESIGN IDEAS

Serge self-fabric band and mock band hems. See pages 69 and 74.

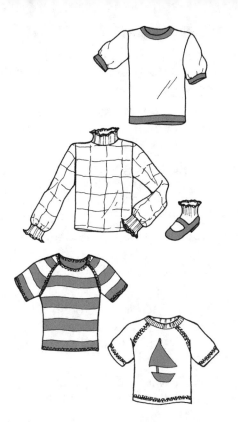

"Lettuce leaf" single or double layer ribbing edges with a medium to narrow satin serge. (See page 75.) "Lettuce leaf" ribbed sock tops to match.

Expose T-shirt seams. See page 60.

Flatlock seams and hems — perfect for piecing, color blocking and soft babywear. See pages 66 and 67.

MAKE FRILLY DRESSES AND BLOUSES SURPRISINGLY FAST!

1. Serge edges of fabric strips for bows and ribbons for ponytails, trims, and ties.
2. Narrow hem ruffle edges with matching or contrasting thread, before gathering.

3. Place collar and sash pieces wrong sides together and finish edges with narrow to medium width satin stitch.
4. Serge pin tucks (see page 80).
5. Serge over $1/16''$-$1/8''$ wide ribbon (see page 65).
6. Gather sleeve caps, skirt waistlines, and ruffle edges with serging (see page 73).
7. Serge on collar without facings (see page 72).

DRESS WAISTLINES WITH ELASTIC

This technique is perfect for dresses with waistline seams. It's fast because the elastic is attached while sewing the waistline seam, all in one step. No casing is necessary.

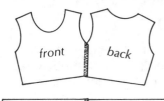

1. Cut ⅜" elastic to fit the waistline comfortably plus 1" extra for seam allowances.

2. Serge the right bodice side seam. Then serge the right skirt side seam.

3. Place bodice and skirt right sides together at waistline. (If skirt must be slightly gathered to fit bodice, do so first.)

4. Place elastic on top of the seam. Overlock through all thicknesses, stretching the elastic in front of the foot to the seam length.

5. With waistline seams up, serge the left side seam and finish dress.

RECEIVING BLANKETS

New moms and kids never have enough! Make them double sided for a pretty, weightier blanket. Buy two 1¼ yard pieces of flannel. Trim to 45" square (conveniently larger than most ready-mades). Place the two squares wrong sides together. Finish the two layers as one with decorative serging (see Chapter 8). We love the look of pearl cotton in the upper and lower loopers (the finest pearl cotton, #8 size works best in the lower looper).

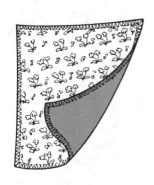

CHAPTER 15

FAST WARDROBE FIX UPS!

Let's face it. Wardrobe fix-ups, like hemming and altering, aren't fun. Yet you and your family could be wearing all those clothes in the "to-be-done" pile. Speed up the process with serging!

SERGED HEMS

Too-short garments can be lengthened by letting down the full hem allowance, and serging the lower edge. Thread shades slightly darker than the fabric produce the least visible serged edges. Use a 2 or 3-thread stitch. For lighter weight fabrics, consider a rolled edge.

The "no-hem" hem is great for shortening or lengthening:

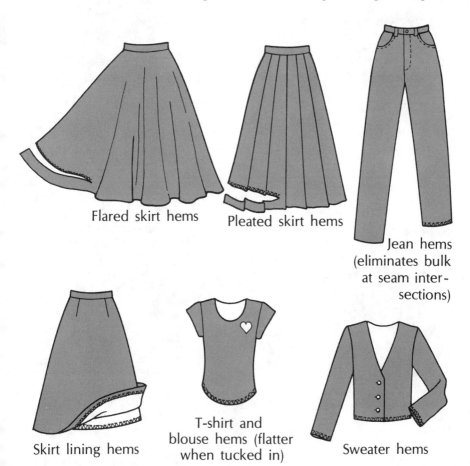

Flared skirt hems

Pleated skirt hems

Jean hems (eliminates bulk at seam inter-sections)

Skirt lining hems

T-shirt and blouse hems (flatter when tucked in)

Sweater hems

Tapering

Need to fit too-full garments? Do it with your serger. Pin fit first. Then, starting at the hem, taper to nothing and chain off, securing threads with sealant. One inch or wider hems should be taken out before tapering. Use this technique for:

- Men's and women's shirts

- Straightening flared or wide leg pants (easiest if originally sewn with serged seams).

- Sweaters

- T-shirts and other casual tops.

Serge Into Patchwork

CHAPTER 16

SERGE INTO PATCHWORK

Sergers can produce beautiful patchwork results in a fraction of the time it takes on a conventional machine. First, the speed of the serger itself makes sewing the endless rows of strips together much faster. Also, you can make unlined patched tops and tablecloths and they will be instantly finished. A serged seam is a finished seam!

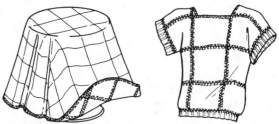

EASY STRIP PATCHING METHOD

1. Cut strips of different colors or designs of fabrics. Stack the fabric and use a rotary cutter (page 30) through several layers at one time.

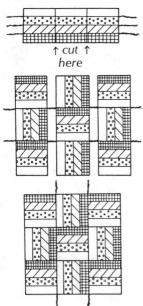

↑ cut ↑
here

2. Serge the strips together with a 3, 3/4, or 4-thread serger. The latter two may be more durable for loosely woven fabrics or patchwork that is to be washed a lot.

3. Cut serged strips into blocks.

4. Rearrange the blocks and serge together forming your patchwork design.

CUT OUT YOUR PATTERN AFTER MAKING PATCHWORK YARDAGE

You can sew a patchwork garment using any pattern by cutting out **after** the patchwork is made. The seams joining the patchwork can be exposed or inside of the garment.

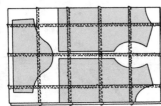

CHAPTER 17

PATTERNLESS QUICK PROJECTS

What can you do with very little time and no pattern? Lots. Just put your serger to work! These patternless projects are penny-wise too. Most can be made in minutes using remnants from your stash. You won't be caught empty-handed the next time you need a gift, or something special to wear. Friends will exclaim, "How did you **ever** find the time?"

ONE-SIZE-FITS-ALL ACCESSORIES

One-step serged edge finishing makes scarves, shawls, mufflers, and any wrap accessory easier than ever to sew. You'll love the professional look of the durable and drapable serged edges. Vary the fabrics, finishing and sizes to create uniquely different looks.

Suggested fabrics: silks (the most drapable and easily tied), silk-likes, lightweight cottons and cotton blends, laces, lightweight wool jersey and rayon or wool challis.

Suggested Sizes (unfinished):

Square Scarves/Shawls:

- Small 10" × 10" (yardage required: only 1/3 yd. of 45"+ width, yields 3 scarves).

- Medium 24" × 24" (yardage required: 3/4 yd. of 45" width yields 2 scarves).

- Large 40" × 40" (yardage required: 1 1/8 yd. of 45"+ width).

- Extra large 45"-60" square (fold in half to wear as shawl) yardage required: (1 1/4 - 1 2/3 yd. of 45-60" width)

Square Scarf

Rectangles:

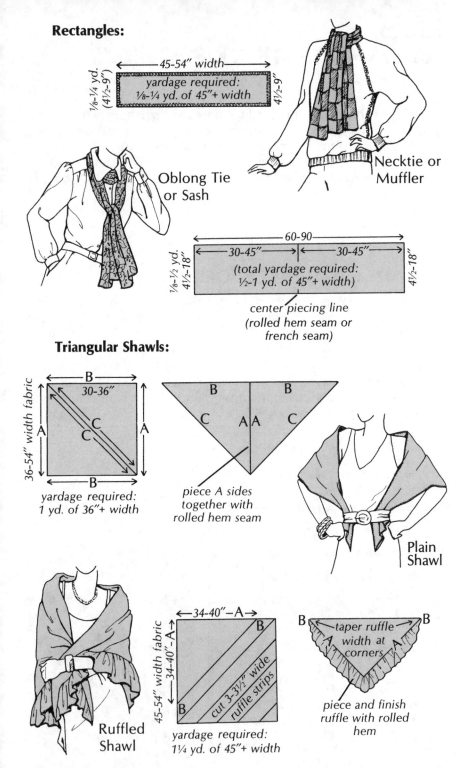

45-54" width

yardage required:
1/8-1/4 yd. of 45"+ width

1/8-1/4 yd.
(4½-9")

4½-9"

Oblong Tie or Sash

Necktie or Muffler

60-90

30-45" | 30-45"

(total yardage required:
½-1 yd. of 45"+ width)

1/8-½ yd.
4½-18"

4½-18"

center piecing line
(rolled hem seam or
french seam)

Triangular Shawls:

B
30-36"

36-54" width fabric

A | A

C
C

B

yardage required:
1 yd. of 36"+ width

B | B

C | A A | C

piece A sides
together with
rolled hem seam

Plain Shawl

Ruffled Shawl

34-40"–A

34-40"–A

45-54" width fabric

B

cut 3-3½" wide
ruffle strips

B | B

yardage required:
1¼ yd. of 45"+ width

B | B

taper ruffle
width at
corners

A | A

piece and finish
ruffle with rolled
hem

114

PATTERNLESS SILKY PULL

A simple, silky "pull," can be made with **only one yard of fabric**. About 40 minutes is all you need for cutting and sewing!

1. Cut two rectangles.

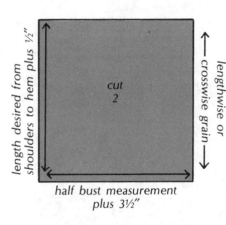

length desired from shoulders to hem plus ½"

lengthwise or crosswise grain

cut 2

half bust measurement plus 3½"

2. Finish both rectangles with serging.

finish with serging (rolled hem or any decorative serging).

3. Pin shoulders and sides wrong sides together or lap front over back ¼" and pin. Try on. Make any fit adjustments necessary.

4. Stitch the two rectangles together.

You're done!

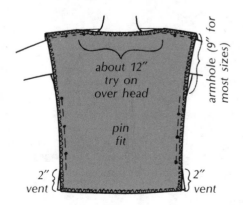

about 12" try on over head

armhole (9" for most sizes)

pin fit

2" vent

2" vent

CHAPTER 18

FAST DECORATING WITH FABRIC

With few exceptions, decorating projects can be seamed and finished entirely with your serger, and in record time. In fact, you'll wonder how you ever managed to decorate without a serger.

narrow rolled hem on curtain

wall quilt with decorative serged edge finish

narrow serged seams in unlined lampshade

serged piecing seams

serged blindstitched hem

gathered ruffle

rolled or narrow unrolled hem

Do-it-yourself decorators will also love the lightweight durability of serged edges, hems, and seams. No more tedious clipping of raveling after laundering.

FABRIC DECORATING TIPS

- Buy 2-3 yards more than you think will be necessary. Decorating projects **always** seem to require more than is estimated. You can use remnants for pillows, tablecloths, lampshades and other accessories. Before you make the substantial multi-yard purchase, buy a "trial" yard. Display it in the room to be redecorated and live with it for a week or so. You'll be better able to decide if the color, print scale, and texture enhance the room, the lighting and your lifestyle.

- Look for the many decorating cut-outs now available by the yard — napkins, placemats, pillow cases, etc. Cut out and finish with your serger in one step!

- Do not prewash most decorator yardage. Because you're not fitting a body, shrinkage is seldom a problem. Besides, pressing all that yardage is incredibly time-consuming.

- Watch for one-way naps, stripes, and prints that make matching necessary. Plot matching BEFORE cutting lengths and seaming.

- Wider width fabrics and sheets minimize piecing. However, sheets are not designed to match at seamlines like decorator prints that match automatically at selvages (like wallpaper).

- Cut out stripes and borders for trims, ruffles, and ties. The savings compared to buying readymade trims are significant! Finish the edges with rolled hem or narrow unrolled satin serging (see pages 43, 74).

SEAMS

A 4-thread stitch is an excellent choice for seaming loosely woven decorator projects. The double chainstitch and wider seam allowances are stabilizing and durable. If you have a 3 or 3/4-thread machine, sew a test seam. If it pulls out when strained, then sew seams first with a straight stitch on your conventional machine and finish with serging.

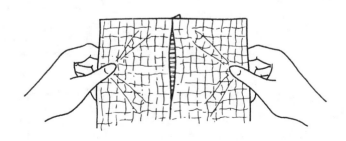

EDGE FINISHING

Finishing furnishings is really not much different from finishing garments . . . in fact, it's easier! Because decorating involves yard after yard of straight edges, projects are perfect for newcomers to serging. You won't have to worry much about curves, corners, or changing thread. Just be sure to buy enough thread!

GATHERS

For gathering ruffles used for trim or dust ruffles, use the gathering technique shown on page 73.

QUICK CREATIVE PROJECTS

Napkins

Edge finish cotton and cotton blend fabrics for napkins. Absolutely no one has enough!! Gail's mother, Betty, entertains constantly and has placed orders for 25 more of one print! Only one yard of 45" width is required for four dinner size 18" × 18" napkins or six smaller 15" × 15" napkins.

Cut out and edge finish at the same time with the serger. Mark napkins with a washable marker. Finish all the lengthwise grain edges first, then the crosswise grain edges. (The lengthwise grain has less tendency to pull out at the corners where the edge finishing intersects.) Chain off at the corners and use seam sealant. There is no need to "turn the corner" on napkins.

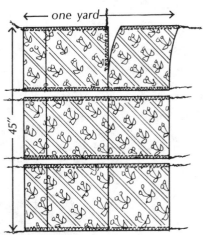

Variation — line napkins with coordinating or contrasting fabric. Edge finish as one layer.

Runners

Runners require less fabric than tablecloths and show off beautiful furniture. Most runners are 12" wide finished and any length you like. If the runners are placed on the table as placemats, cut them wide enough to be 16" finished.

Cut out runner fabric on either the crosswise or lengthwise grain. If piecing, the seam should fall in the center of the runner. Corners can be rounded for continuous serging. Or, leave as is, chain off and secure threads with seam sealant.

Variations: Line to add body, reversibility, and quilt the runner. Sandwich a layer of polyester fleece between the runner and lining. Edge finish as one layer, serging the longer sides first, then the short ends. Then channel quilt with a straight stitch. Space stitching lines 2-3" apart and alternate the direction of stitching to prevent pulling and puckering.

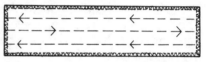

Placemats

You will never go back to binding placemats again! Buy quilted fabric or preprinted placemat yardage. Just one yard of 45" fabric will yield six 16 × 14" placemats. Measure and mark placemats on yardage with a washable marker. Cut, rounding out corners for faster finishing. (Use a glass or a cup for nice round corners.) Serge finish edges with a close wide stitch. (For neat "serging in a circle," see page 45). Go around the placemat twice if necessary for increased thread coverage. Decorative threads like pearl cotton give good coverage also.

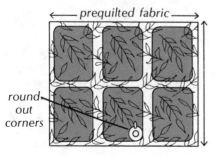

← prequilted fabric →

round out corners

Tablecloths

If necessary, piece fabric using your serger. Put cloth on table to mark length. Using a narrow or rolled edge, serge finish the hemline and say goodbye to tedious hemming. Even round tablecloths are quick to sew.

Washcloths and towels

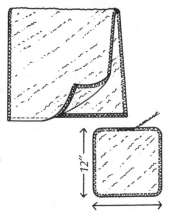

We would **never** have considered sewing these bathroom essentials before discovering sergers. Now, with the help of this new sewing technology, washcloths and towels are a snap!

Use your readymade washclothes (most are 12" × 12") and towels as patterns, or look up dimensions in mail order catalogues.

Most washcloths have rounded corners making serging easier. Towels are generally rectangular. Serge from the center of one side all the way around to about 2" over your first line of stitching (see page 45 for neat "serging a circle." If there are corners, serge off each edge and secure corners with seam sealant.

Blankets and afghans

Make blankets easily, quickly and inexpensively out of wool yardage. Look up sizes in mail order catalogues or use one you own as a pattern. Finish edges with serging, using yarn, pearl cotton or other decorative threads.

Worn quilts and blankets can be sectioned into smaller covers for children or for dolls.

Batting and foam filled furnishings

Most sergers can easily stitch through the bulk of two layers fabric plus a layer of ¼"-¾" foam or polyester fleece.

Sandwich the foam between the wrong sides of the fabric and finish the edges with short, wide serging stitch. For chair cushions, attach ties to the corners as you are finishing.

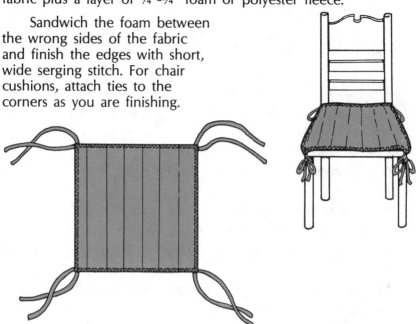

Lampshades

Once a time consuming hand stitched project, serging makes lampshades easier and prettier than ever. Serging also eliminates the need for lining, because seams look good enough to be exposed.

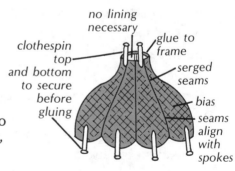

no lining necessary

clothespin top and bottom to secure before gluing

glue to frame

serged seams

bias

seams align with spokes

Because the lampshade frame will show, we recommend spray painting it to coordinate with the fabric **wrong** side. Lay out lampshade pattern. (Most frames come with a pattern. If not, most general fabric decorating books will show you how to make a pattern.) Cut your fabric on the bias so it will have enough give to stretch over the frame. Machine baste the pieces together, fit on the frame, then serge the seams. Seams should align with frame spokes. Glue the top and bottom allowances to the frame.

CHAPTER 19

NIFTY SERGER NOTION CHECKLIST

These notions help make serger sewing even more efficient, easy and fun!

Auxiliary lights — see page 21

Attachable magnifying lens — to magnify threading and stitching

Compressed air — to keep it clean — see page 54

Extension table — for creating a flat surface up and around the serging area

Glue stick — see page 35

Masking tape or Tape Stitch Sewing Tape™ — see page 34

Metal measuring gauge for gauging seam allowances while serging

Needle threaders to assist threading hand or machine needles

Needle-nose pliers for easy, straight insertion of serger needles

Oil and lint brush — see page 54

Rotary cutter and cutting mat — see page 30

Screw drivers for changing stitch length — see page 18

Seam ripper — see page 40

Seam sealant (Fray Check™ and Fray-No-More™) — see page 38

Serger knives — see page 20

Serger needles in a range of sizes — see page 20

Serger tweezers — long bent shape that comes with your machine (replacements also available in notions departments)

Thread, decorative, coned or tubed — see pages 23-26

Tote bag — specially designed for carrying your serger

Washable markers (water soluble or air erasable) — see pages 31, 34

CHAPTER 20
DIFFERENTIAL FEED

To understand the term "differential feed," you must first understand the term "feed dog." Feed dogs are sets of metal "teeth" built into a sewing machine or serger below the presser foot. They grab fabric, move it along, then sink below the throat plate and move toward the front of the machine and up to begin again. There may be one or more sets, but all move at the same rate.

WHAT IS DIFFERENTIAL FEED?

Differential feed dogs are TWO sets of teeth, one in front of the other. The speed of the front feed dog is controlled by a dial or lever with three settings, 0.7, 1 and 2.

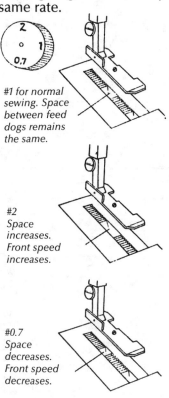

#1 for normal sewing. Space between feed dogs remains the same.

With differential feed set on number 2, the front feed dog moves twice as much fabric under the presser foot as the rear feed dog lets out, creating a gathering or "easing" effect. This prevents stretch and is great for sweaterknits.

#2 Space increases. Front speed increases.

With differential feed set on number 0.7, the front feed dog will move seven tenths as much fabric under the presser foot as the rear feed dog lets out, creating a "stretching" effect.

#0.7 Space decreases. Front speed decreases.

WHERE TO USE DIFFERENTIAL FEED

Set differential feed on 2 and you can keep sweaterknits from stretching. You can also gather lightweight fabrics. For maximum gathering, also lengthen your stitch. If you are easing one layer into another, as when sewing a sleeve to an armhole, put the layer you are easing nearest the feed dogs. You can finish the edge of a circle skirt and prevent it from stretching and becoming wavy all at the same time with differential feed set on 2.

With differential feed set on 0.7 you can prevent puckers in silkies. We use it to prevent puckers when sewing a rolled edge on a lightweight fabric or the crossgrain on napkins.

CHAPTER 21
FAVORITE STITCHES

For convenient reference, make note of special machine settings and thread types used for your favorite stitches.

(tape sample here)	*(tape sample here)*

Comments: _____
_____
_____
_____
_____

Comments: _____
_____
_____
_____
_____

(tape sample here)	*(tape sample here)*

Comments: _____
_____
_____
_____
_____

Comments: _____
_____
_____
_____
_____

Store where machine was purchased _____
Dealer's Phone Number: _____ Date _____

*(tape
sample
here)*

*(tape
sample
here)*

Comments: _____
_____
_____
_____
_____

Comments: _____
_____
_____
_____
_____

*(tape
sample
here)*

*(tape
sample
here)*

Comments: _____
_____
_____
_____
_____

Comments: _____
_____
_____
_____
_____

INDEX

More Products from Palmer/Pletsch

Look for these easy-to-use, information-filled sewing books and videos in local fabric stores, or contact us for ordering information.

Books available spiral bound— add $3.00 for large books, $2.00 for small.

8½ x 11 BOOKS:

☐ **Dream Sewing Spaces** *by Lynette Ranney Black.* Make your dream a reality. Analyze your needs and your space, then learn to plan and put it together. Lots of color photos! *128 pgs., $19.95*

☐ **The BUSINE$$ of Teaching Sewing,** *by Marcy Miller and Pati Palmer.* How to be a great teacher. How to run a home-based teaching business. How to make money doing what you love. *128 pgs., $29.95 (no spiral)*

☐ **Couture—The Art of Fine Sewing,** *by Roberta C. Carr.* How-to's of couture techniques and secrets, with illustrations and dozens of garments photographed in full color. *208 pgs., $29.95*

☐ **The Serger Idea Book—A Collection of Inspiring Ideas from Palmer/Pletsch.** Color photos and how-to's on inspiring and fashionable ideas from the Extraordinary to the Practical. *160 pgs., $19.95*

☐ **Creative Serging for the Home and Other Quick Decorating Ideas,** *by Lynette Ranney Black and Linda Wisner.* Color photos and how-to's to help you transform your home into the place you want it to be. *160 pgs., $18.95*

☐ **Sewing Ultrasuede® Brand Products** *by Marta Alto, Pati Palmer and Barbara Weiland.* Fashion photo section, plus the newest techniques to master these luxurious fabrics. *128 pgs., $16.95*

And coming in 1996:
☐ **Fit For Real People**

MY FIRST SEWING BOOK KITS

by Winky Cherry. A series of learn-to-sew book kits for children ages 5 to 11: hand sewing, embroidery, doll making, and machine sewing. *$12.95 each.* Teaching materials available. Ask for our Children's Catalog.

VIDEOS—$29.95 each (VHS only)
☐ **Sewing the Time Saving Way** (45 min.)
☐ **Sewing to Success** (45 min.)
☐ **Sewing With Sergers — Basics** (1 hr.)
☐ **Sewing With Sergers — Advanced** (1 hr.)
☐ **Creative Serging** (1 hr.)
☐ **Creative Serging II** (1 hr.)
☐ **Sewing With Ultrasuede** (1 hr.)
☐ **Creative Home Decorating Ideas** (69 min.)
☐ **2-Hour Trousers** (1 hr., 40 min.)

5½ x 8½ BOOKS:

☐ **Sewing With Sergers—The Complete Handbook for Overlock Sewing,** *by Pati Palmer and Gail Brown.* Learn easy threading tips, stitch types, rolled edging and flatlocking on your serger. *128 pgs., Revised Edition $8.95*

☐ **Creative Serging—The Complete Handbook for Decorative Overlock Sewing,** *by Pati Palmer, Gail Brown and Sue Green.* Indepth information and creative uses of your serger. *128 pgs., $8.95*

☐ **Sew To Success!—How to Make Money in a Home-Based Sewing Business,** *by Kathleen Spike.* Learn how to establish your market, set policies and procedures, price your talents and more! *128 pgs., $10.95*

☐ **Mother Pletsch's Painless Sewing,** *NEW Revised Edition, by Pati Palmer and Susan Pletsch.* The most uncomplicated sewing book of the century! Filled with sewing tips to sew FAST! *128 pgs., $8.95*

☐ **Pants For Any Body,** *Revised Edition, by Pati Palmer and Susan Pletsch.* Learn to fit pants with clear step-by-step problem and solution illustrations. *128 pgs., $8.95*

☐ **Easy, Easier, Easiest Tailoring,** *Revised Edition, by Pati Palmer and Susan Pletsch.* Learn 4 different tailoring methods, easy fit tips, and timesaving machine lining. *128 pgs., $8.95*

☐ **Sensational Silk—A Handbook for Sewing Silk and Silk-like Fabrics,** *by Gail Brown.* Complete guide for sewing with silk and silkies plus all kinds of great blouse and dress techniques. *128 pgs., $8.95*

☐ **Sew a Beautiful Wedding,** *by Gail Brown and Karen Dillon.* Bridal how-to's from choosing the most flattering style to sewing with specialty fabrics. *128 pgs., $8.95*

We also offer workshops and teacher training, **Perfect Sew Wash-Away Fabric Stabilizer and needle threader**, plus hard-to-find decorative threads.

Palmer/Pletsch Associates
P.O. Box 12046, Portland, OR 97212-0046
(503) 274-0687/ORDERS: 1-800-728-3784

International orders please pay in U.S. funds or with Visa or MasterCard. Shipping and handling: ($1–13.99) $2.50; ($14–24.99) $2.75; ($25–49.99) $3.00; ($50+) $4.00. Please allow 4–6 weeks for delivery.